ENDORSEMENTS

"Few books aimed at self-help and motivation — even good ones — ever really result in the readers' sustained behavior modification or an explosion of self-image and potential. Skot has created a unique system of transformation in his short, 52-chapter book, including a self-feedback tracking loop to inspire you to take action. This isn't just another self-help book but rather a structured, irresistible path of inspiration that will kick your self-confidence into gear, stimulating you to lead yourself into greatness."

FRANK O'CONNELL / FORMER CEO OF INDIAN MOTORCYCLES AND GIBSON GREETINGS, INC., AND FORMER PRESIDENT OF REEBOK BRANDS AND HBO VIDEO

"Skot is amazing. He not only inspires you to get Unlocked, he gives you a game plan to do it. Leverage this book for your benefit!"

JEREMIE KUBICEK, BEST-SELLING AUTHOR, SPEAKER, AND CO-FOUNDER OF GIANT

"Skot Waldron's *Unlocked* brilliantly distills the essence of intentional leadership into a year-long journey of self-discovery and empowerment. This book is an invaluable tool for anyone aspiring to lead with authenticity and impact."

STEVE COCKRAM, BEST-SELLING AUTHOR, SPEAKER, AND CO-FOUNDER OF GIANT

"*Unlocked* brilliantly maps an actionable, week-by-week journey of self-growth. You are about to believe in yourself like you never have before."

MIKE MICHALOWICZ, AUTHOR OF ALL IN AND PROFIT FIRST

"In *Unlocked,* Skot Waldron provides a fantastic set list to weekly self-discovery. Each chapter offers up practical and tactical applications along with the space to craft a customized path to intentional leadership. This is transformation that rocks!"

JIM KNIGHT, TOP 10 KEYNOTE SPEAKER & BESTSELLING AUTHOR, CULTURE THAT ROCKS

"Just as a journey of a thousand miles begins with a single step, author Skot Waldron leads us on a 52-week leadership journey of exploration and discovery, conveniently breaking down a year's worth of leadership lessons into easy-to-digest, one-week-at-a-time, bite-sized pieces that will engage and inspire you every step of the way."

TODD CHERCHES, CEO OF BIGBLUEGUMBALL, AND AUTHOR OF VISUALEADERSHIP: LEVERAGING THE POWER OF VISUAL THINKING IN LEADERSHIP AND IN LIFE

"Leadership development is a journey no one successfully achieves alone. Skot Waldron's Unlocked offers a unique transformation system through small, intentional actions. This book, this system, is clearly defined as your climbing partner as you endeavor to ascend on the most important journey of your life. Each chapter can be read in just a few minutes, yet the effects become life-changing when the prompts are followed."

DOV BARON, ARCHITECT OF THE EMOTIONAL SOURCE CODE, THE SCIENCE OF EMOTION, TOP 100 LEADERSHIP SPEAKER, TOP 30 GLOBAL LEADERSHIP GURU, BESTSELLING AUTHOR

"Personal growth isn't automatic but is accelerated with assets like intent, structure, and consistency. *Unlocked*, by Skot Waldron, provides all three growth assets in one work to help you discover the greater you within you.

DAVE ANDERSON, PRESIDENT LEARNTOLEAD, AUTHOR, "INTENTIONAL MINDSET."

"*Unlocked* is not just a great book. It is a great, year-long Master Class for everyone that is ready to transform into the best version of themselves through inspiration, self-discovery, and life mastery."

GREG MUZZILLO, FOUNDER OF PROFORMA

UNLOCKED

A 52-Week Guide for
THE INTENTIONAL LEADER

SKOT WALDRON

WALDO
PUBLISHING

FOREWORD BY DR. MARK GOULSTON

In the landscape of personal development and professional growth, there comes along every so often a book that doesn't just tell you what to do but reaches inside you and changes how you think, feel, and perceive the world. Unlocked is one such book that has the potential to quietly revolutionize your life.

From my experience as a therapist, I have learned that change, growth, and healing often begin with a new understanding, a different perspective, or a small but significant shift in how we approach our inner and outer worlds. This book guides you through a journey that isn't just about the surface-level mechanics of success but about the deeper, more fulfilling aspects of what it means to lead a life that truly matters—not just to yourself but to the people around you.

Skot doesn't just scratch the surface of self-improvement; he delves deeper into the heart of what makes us tick as human beings. Through a blend of personal anecdotes, real-life examples, and actionable advice, he invites you to look within and ask the hard questions to engage in the kind of self-reflection that is often uncomfortable but always invaluable.

As you turn the pages, you'll find that each chapter is a step towards a more empowered, insightful self. The challenges and principles outlined here are strategies and stepping stones to a more profound self-awareness and an authentic way of living and leading.

In my book, *Just Listen*, I explore the transformative power of being heard and understanding others. In *Unlocked*, you are invited to listen not just to the words on the page but to your own inner voice, the one that's been waiting for you to pay attention and harness its wisdom for your growth and contentment.

So, as you embark on this journey, keep your mind open, your heart ready to learn, and your spirit willing to be transformed. The steps you are about to take can lead to not just incremental changes but leaps in your personal and professional life. Here's to your success as you define it, and as you live it.

I wish you the best,
Dr. Mark Goulston

Let's Begin

INTRODUCTION

INTRODUCTION

You're about to embark on an extraordinary journey, an expedition that will lead you not across continents but deep into the vast landscapes of your own self-awareness, self-love, and self-leadership. It's a quest destined to redefine your understanding of yourself and transform your engagement with the world around you.

This book isn't just a silent observer of your evolution. It's a catalyst for transformation, making you more aware of the power of intentionality. You'll uncover the essence of the person you are today while unlocking the extraordinary potential of who you will become in the (near) future through small, intentional actions. Massive change occurs through millions of micro-moments in life, not necessarily through grand gestures.

Consider this journey a conversation between your present and future selves. It's not just about self-discovery, but also about self-creation. It's about recognizing the precious gem that you are already and then meticulously refining, polishing, and reshaping that gem into something even more precious.

True transformation isn't comfortable. In fact, it demands discomfort. There will be moments of joy and revelation, coupled with periods of discipline and challenges. It's through these experiences, the comfortable and the uncomfortable, that you will grow, evolve, and truly come into your own. So, stay with me! It's this continual dance between comfort and growth that fosters your transformation, guiding you toward realizing your full potential and embracing the best version of yourself.

Remember that, as someone somewhere once said, "Growth never happens in the comfort zone, and comfort doesn't exist in the growth zone." So, brace yourself for a little discomfort.

Each chapter of this book represents a week's journey, a week filled with introspection, reflection, and purposeful action. You'll delve into thought-provoking questions, ponder meaningful quotes, and engage in activities, all meticulously designed to help you uncover your strengths, confront your weaknesses, and cultivate your leadership abilities. You will become better. A better what, you ask? A better boss, a better employee, a better parent, a better sibling, a better... human.

This book is about both you and the impact you can have on others. We'll focus on your development first, then we'll move on to how you can lead others more intentionally and therefore create the influence and legacy you desire.

And here's the beauty of it all: this journey isn't a race. It's a delicate, patient exploration of your inner landscape, a quest marked by gradual, consistent steps toward personal growth and understanding. As you navigate this path week by week, you'll witness the subtle shifts, the emerging patterns, the increase in self-love, and the empowering self-leadership that grows within you.

So, strap on your metaphorical boots and pack your spirit with curiosity, courage, and a willingness to embrace vulnerability. This book is not just your guide, it's your compass, your map, and your lantern as you journey into the thrilling depths of self-discovery. Let's take a deep, collective breath, open our hearts wide, and step bravely onto this path of transformation.

Welcome to the journey.

GOAL

Why did you pick up this book?

What's your goal for the next year as you follow the prompts in this book?

When (not if) you encounter challenges along the way, how will you address them?

How will you know you've accomplished your goal?

BASELINE

The tools mentioned in this chapter will be used each time you measure progress throughout your journey. My friends and colleagues Jeremie Kubicek and Steve Cockram, founders of GiANT Worldwide, created them and have graciously allowed me to include them in this book. I've used these tools for years to coach and guide my own clients. They will benefit you too. Be honest in your evaluation.

THE TWO SIDES OF LEADERSHIP

Rate yourself from 1-10, with 1 being the lowest and 10 being the highest:

RATE HOW WELL YOU'RE PERSONALLY PERFORMING:

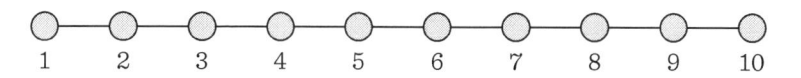

O—O—O—O—O—O—O—O—O—O
1   2   3   4   5   6   7   8   9   10

RATE HOW WELL YOU'RE LEADING PERFORMERS:

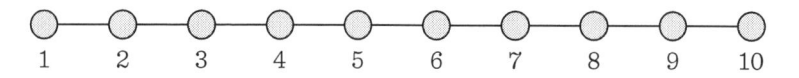

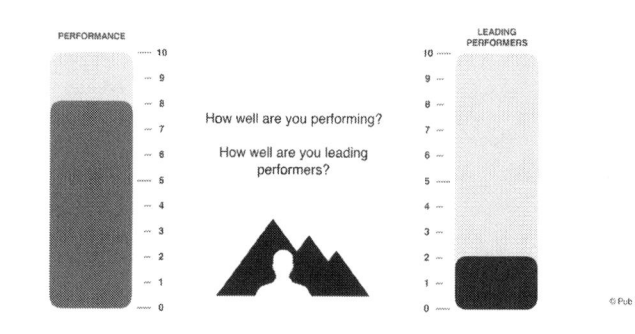

O—O—O—O—O—O—O—O—O—O
1   2   3   4   5   6   7   8   9   10

PERFORMANCE | LEADING PERFORMERS

How well are you performing?

How well are you leading performers?

GiANT © Pub House

INTRODUCTION

SUPPORT AND CHALLENGE

Our goal should be to liberate those we live and work with, which means we fight for their highest possible good. To truly liberate those around us, we need to balance both true support and effective challenges.

Examples of effective support may include training, mentorship, spending time with them, talking about potential, offering words of encouragement, listening, etc.

Naturally, we may be good at offering support but back away from ruffling feathers, confrontation, or challenging others. This can create a culture of entitlement and mistrust.

Examples of effective challenging may include holding people accountable, clarifying expectations, helping people step outside of their comfort zones, follow-ups, setting goals, having difficult conversations, etc.

If we're really good at offering challenges without true support, we don't spend time training and mentoring, we aren't vulnerable, we make threats, or we bulldoze meetings and ideas. This can lead to a culture of fear and manipulation.

If we aren't offering support or challenges, then we may be abdicating our responsibilities, leading to a culture of apathy and low expectations. People wonder if they should even care because it appears that we don't.

Liberators. That's what we want to be. When we liberate, we offer support (people know we're for them, not ourselves), and we aren't afraid to hold them accountable. We push people outside of their comfort zone into the growth zone using encouragement and trust. This is where influence and legacy are built.

SO, HOW HAVE YOU BEEN SHOWING UP LATELY?

Using the graphic below, plot yourself on the matrix. Make five dots on the illustration below. One for each circle of influence in your life (self, family, team, organization, community). You may want to add a separate dot for each family member or team member. It's up to you. You should have at least five dots at the end of the exercise. Inside of which quadrant do you find most of your dots? Do you tend to be more of a protector, abdicator, dominator, or liberator when it comes to how you engage with others?

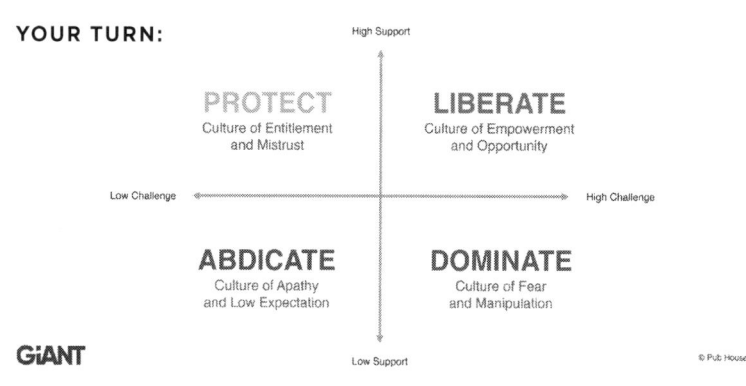

EXAMPLE:

	High Support	
● FAMILY		
PROTECT		**LIBERATE**
Culture of Entitlement and Mistrust		Culture of Empowerment and Opportunity
		● COMMUNITY
Low Challenge	←――――――――――→	High Challenge
ORGANIZATION ●	● SELF	
ABDICATE		**DOMINATE**
Culture of Apathy and Low Expectation		Culture of Fear and Manipulation
TEAM ●		
	Low Support	

GiANT © Pub House

YOUR TURN:

	High Support	
PROTECT		**LIBERATE**
Culture of Entitlement and Mistrust		Culture of Empowerment and Opportunity
Low Challenge	←――――――――――→	High Challenge
ABDICATE		**DOMINATE**
Culture of Apathy and Low Expectation		Culture of Fear and Manipulation
	Low Support	

GiANT © Pub House

KNOW, LOVE, LEAD

Rate yourself on a scale of 1-10 on how well you know yourself, how much you love yourself, and how well you lead yourself, with 1 being the lowest score and 10 being the highest.

KNOW:

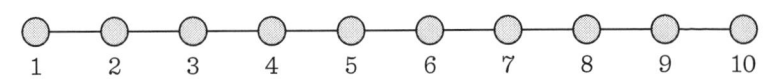

○——○——○——○——○——○——○——○——○——○
1   2   3   4   5   6   7   8   9   10

LOVE:

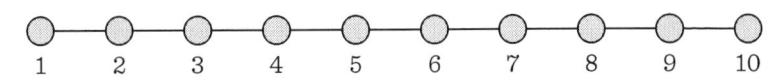

○——○——○——○——○——○——○——○——○——○
1   2   3   4   5   6   7   8   9   10

LEAD:

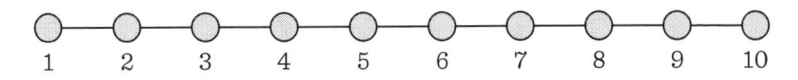

○——○——○——○——○——○——○——○——○——○
1   2   3   4   5   6   7   8   9   10

> **THESE ARE TWO TOOLS OUT OF 60+ THAT I USE TO COACH MY CLIENTS. GAIN ACCESS TO ALL OF THEM AT WWW.SKOTWALDRON.COM/TOOLS.**

Part One

KNOW YOURSELF

WEEK 1

CHALLENGES DIMINISH IN SIZE WHEN VIEWED THROUGH THE LENS OF COMPANIONSHIP.

INSPIRATION

Picture this: you're standing at the foot of a massive mountain. Could you tackle that climb solo? Maybe, you've got the spirit and determination. But what if you had a friend strapped into their climbing gear beside you? Suddenly, that looming peak doesn't feel so daunting, does it? Instead of a solo endeavor, it's a shared adventure. And here's the kicker—studies show this isn't just a feel-good concept; sharing the challenge reshapes the way you perceive it.

A classic study on this matter is from Shelley E. Taylor's "Tend-and-Befriend" theory, where she discusses how humans, particularly females, tend to band together and support each other in stressful times. This contrasts with the "fight-or-flight" response traditionally associated with stress. In this context, having someone else around during a challenge (like climbing a mountain) might trigger feelings of safety and shared purpose, thereby reducing the perceived difficulty of the task.[1]

In another study, two researchers in Virginia found that when looking alone at a hill, it can look 20% steeper than when you view that hill standing next to someone who is going to climb it with you.[2]

I'll be the first to tell you that I need accountability. I love having someone checking up on me. As I've come to know myself better, I've learned that integrity is a huge thing for me. I expect it from others, and I expect it from myself. This is why having someone with me is great motivation. If I commit, if I tell someone else I'm all in, then I tend to hold to that promise.

So, let's bring this concept back down to earth and into our everyday lives. This book you're holding? Consider it your metaphorical mountain. And while you can trek solo, I invite you to consider finding an accountability partner for this journey.

Why? Having someone to share your discoveries with, to celebrate your progress, and to keep you focused when the terrain gets tough can make all the difference. So, as you embark on this transformative journey, consider who in your life might be ready for this climb, too. After all, the triumphs are even sweeter when shared. Let's create an environment where we aren't just scaling heights individually but lifting each other up to reach our peaks. Here's to shared adventures and collective victories.

APPLICATION

> Do you tend to take things on alone or reach out to others when a new challenge arises?

> What are you going to do to feel less alone on your journey this week? One suggestion is to find someone to take it with you.

Invite someone else on the journey with you. Rather go alone? No problem. Send a message to someone, anyone, and tell them what you're doing.

> When are you going to take action?

Tell, text, or share this with your accountability partner or someone else.

TRANSFORMATION

Did you invite someone to join you or tell someone what you're doing?

○ Yes ○ No

Did you share this week's Inspiration, Application, or Transformation with someone?

○ Yes ○ No

If not, do it now.

Did you kick this thing off well and complete your goal?

○ Yes ○ No

> If not, what got in the way of you completing your goal?

---

[1] Taylor, Shelley. "Tend and Befriend Theory." 22 Oct. 2014, taylorlab.psych.ucla.edu/wp-content/uploads/sites/5/2014/11/2011_Tend-and-Befriend-Theory.pdf. Accessed 23 Oct. 2023.

[2] Schnall S, Harber KD, Stefanucci JK, Proffitt DR. "Social Support and the Perception of Geographical Slant." *J Exp Soc Psychol*. 2008 Sep 1;44(5):1246-1255. doi: 10.1016/j.jesp.2008.04.011. PMID: 22389520; PMCID: PMC3291107.

WEEK 2

IT'S NOT THE LOAD THAT BREAKS YOU DOWN, IT'S THE WAY YOU CARRY IT.

LOU HOLTZ

INSPIRATION

Picture life as an endless whirl of activities, responsibilities, and decisions. We often find ourselves more spectators than drivers. Without realizing it, you can be adrift without a compass, simply trying to stay on the right path amidst life's currents.

And then there's survival mode—ever been there? That's when you're just getting by, meeting the demands of each day, but hardly pausing to refuel. Taking time to recharge can feel like a luxury you can't afford. Some may even see it as self-indulgence or an unproductive pause in the hustle.

Not taking the time to recharge leads to burnout. Burnout has three main dimensions: emotional exhaustion (feeling overextended and drained), depersonalization (a cynical and detached attitude towards one's job or clients/customers), and reduced personal accomplishment (feeling incompetent and unproductive at work).[1] It has also been linked to numerous health issues, including cardiovascular diseases, immune disorders, insomnia, and depression.

No thanks. Let's choose the "recharge" option instead.

Making recharging a routine part of your life is the secret to maintaining your well-being. It's like a super vitamin for your soul, a nourishing element that replenishes your energy, both at home and in the professional space. Give yourself permission to incorporate rest and renewal into your daily rhythm—it's an investment that pays dividends in every aspect of your life.

APPLICATION

> **What's one thing you like to do to recharge, and when was the last time you did that?**
> *Recharging can happen alone or with someone else. It can involve reading a book or hiking a mountain. It can be daily or weekly. No rules.*

> **What are you going to do to recharge this week? When in doubt, schedule it.**

> **When are you going to take action?**

Tell, text, or share this with your accountability partner or someone else.

TRANSFORMATION

> What tendencies got in the way of your recharge
> or enabled you to make it happen?

Do you know yourself better this week than you did last week?

◯ Yes ◯ No

Did you share this week's Inspiration, Application, or Transformation with someone?

◯ Yes ◯ No

If not, do it now.

Did you complete your goal?

◯ Yes ◯ No

---

[1]Maslach, C., Schaufeli, W. B., & Leiter, M. P. (2001). "Job burnout." *Annual Review of Psychology,* 52(1), 397-422.

WEEK 3

YOUR DISCOMFORT CAN HELP CREATE SOMEONE ELSE'S COMFORT. IT'S UP TO YOU TO DETERMINE IF IT'S WORTH IT. USUALLY, IT IS.

BRENDON BURCHARD

INSPIRATION

We're wired to crave comfort, aren't we? Adjusting the thermostat, quenching our thirst, or even that divine quest for the perfect pair of hiking boots that won't result in blisters.

What about when we are asked to take extra time to listen or help someone in need, or spend our Saturday helping someone move? Funny how those things don't usually come at times that are convenient for us.

I love being comfortable. Or maybe I hate being uncomfortable? I don't know if that tendency will ever go away. But the more I experience that feeling, the more familiar I am with it. And the more I push through that feeling, especially when it comes to doing things for others, the more I realize that once I've completed that task, the reward far exceeds the discomfort.

The brain naturally seeks pleasure and avoids pain. This is largely regulated by the brain's reward system. When you encounter uncomfortable situations, your brain doesn't release the "feel-good" neurotransmitters, such as dopamine, making the experience less enticing.

As you step out of your comfort zone to help, you not only discover new facets of yourself but also become more empathetic and understanding of others. By navigating your own discomfort, you develop the resilience and insights needed to effectively support those around you, fostering a collaborative environment that empowers everyone to learn, adapt, and thrive together.

APPLICATION

Who is one person you can go out of your way to help this week? It should make you a little uncomfortable.

When are you going to reach out to them?

Tell, text, or share this with your accountability partner or someone else.

TRANSFORMATION

> What tendencies did you experience as you moved
> into an uncomfortable space?

Do you know yourself better this week than you did last week?

○ Yes ○ No

Did you share this week's Inspiration, Application, or Transformation with someone?

○ Yes ○ No

If not, do it now.

Did you complete your goal?

○ Yes ○ No

WEEK 4

BLAME CREATES DISEMPOWERMENT, AND RESPONSIBILITY CREATES EMPOWERMENT. ARE YOU BLAMING OR TAKING RESPONSIBILITY?

JOHN ASSARAF

INSPIRATION

Ever noticed how blame has got a way of saying, "I'm not the boss here," or "I'm just the puppet, not the puppeteer"? It's like a cloak we hide under when things get a bit too real. We try to make ourselves invisible.

But responsibility? Now that's a different story. Responsibility struts in, exclaiming, "I'm in the driver's seat!" It acknowledges the choices we make and empowers us to realize we're the actors, not just spectators in our own stories.

In her book *Mindset: The New Psychology of Success,* Dr. Carol Dweck explains that one of the fundamental distinctions between blame and responsibility is their temporal focus. Blame tends to be retrospective, always looking backward to pinpoint the cause of a past event or mistake. In contrast, responsibility is more prospective, looking ahead to solutions and improvements, and preventing future errors.

Here's the truth, though. Blame is an unsavory companion, often tagging along with insecurity, arrogance, and a big ol' bag of pride. It's a slippery slope that gets you nowhere fast.

Responsibility, on the other hand, is the real deal. It walks hand in hand with security, confidence, and a healthy dose of humility. It's the key that unlocks your potential and paves the way for growth.

APPLICATION

> Who are you blaming right now?

> What part of the situation can you own?

Tell, text, or share this with your accountability partner or someone else.

TRANSFORMATION

> What did it feel like to take responsibility?

Do you know yourself better this week than you did last week?

○ Yes ○ No

Did you share this week's Inspiration, Application, or Transformation with someone?

○ Yes ○ No

If not, do it now.

Did you complete your goal?

○ Yes ○ No

WEEK 5

IT'S REALLY HARD TO RIDE A BIKE THAT ISN'T MOVING. GET STARTED, AND THINGS BECOME EASIER.

ROBERT G. ALLEN

INSPIRATION

Setting off on any expedition, that first step can feel quite heavy. Remember when you first hopped on a bike? That itch to plant your foot on solid ground, the safety net to avoid a topple, was nearly irresistible. Funny enough, it's that same security blanket that hinders us from experiencing the thrill of moving forward.

Before starting a new or unfamiliar task, the brain tends to overestimate the effort required, which can prevent us from taking that first step. Brain sabotage! But once you begin a task, and as you progress, the perceived effort often decreases. This suggests that the brain's initial calculations of effort can be more severe than the actual experience.[1]

Oh, the joy when you finally say goodbye to that anchor and propel ahead. Hair fluttering in the wind, gears shifting effortlessly. It's this unstoppable force, this power of momentum, that removes obstacles and fuels your journey toward personal growth and victory. It's when you get those wheels turning and keep pedaling no matter what that you truly discover your potential and start making tracks on your path of self-discovery.

APPLICATION

What do you need to start doing that
you've been putting off?

What are you going to do about it?

Tell, text, or share this with your accountability partner or someone else.

TRANSFORMATION

....

> What tendencies did you experience as
> you began to "pedal your bike"?

Do you know yourself better this week than you did last week?

◯ Yes ◯ No

Did you share this week's Inspiration, Application, or Transformation with someone?

◯ Yes ◯ No

If not, do it now.

Did you complete your goal?

◯ Yes ◯ No

[1]Vlaev, I., Chater, N., Stewart, N., & Brown, G. D. (2011). "Does the brain calculate value?" *Trends in Cognitive Sciences,* 15(11), 546-554.

WEEK 6

90% PERFECT ON PAPER ALWAYS BEATS 100% PERFECT STUCK IN YOUR HEAD. GIVE US WHAT'S GREAT. DON'T MAKE US WAIT FOR WHAT'S PERFECT.

JON ACUFF

INSPIRATION

Many of us have experienced the relentless pursuit of perfection - that captivating siren song that keeps us from launching our masterpieces into the world. It's a profound realization that perfection can indeed be the nemesis of progression. The real treasure isn't in perfection but in sharing. By offering what's already great, we inspire others, contribute to collective growth, and cultivate an environment that celebrates the journey rather than an unattainable destination of perfection.

A study found that individuals who scored high on perfectionistic traits had an increased fear of failure. This fear often comes from a deeper fear of experiencing shame or embarrassment. About 62% of the participants with high scores in perfectionism showcased tendencies to hold back from sharing their work or achievements compared to just 29% of those with low perfectionistic tendencies.[1] Notice how it didn't say, "Those with zero perfectionistic traits"? Perfectionism tends to hitch itself to all of our backpacks at some point.

By holding back out of fear, you often miss out on valuable feedback, opportunities to learn, and the joy of sharing your achievements with others.

Chasing perfection is like chasing a mirage—you'll never catch it. When you're obsessed with being flawless, you're setting yourself up for a cycle of stress and missed expectations. You're always anxious about proving your worth and can't stop dwelling on your mistakes or what you "should have" done.

Advocate perseverance, flexibility, and diligence. These traits are not only valuable, but they're also a lot healthier for your mindset. Sure, there are times when attention to detail is essential, but aiming for perfection can freeze you in your tracks. Set realistic, attainable goals rather than striving for something as elusive as perfection, and you'll find it's a lot easier to move forward.

In the grand scheme of things, it's all about making things happen rather than making them perfect.

APPLICATION

What process, thought, or project is 90% there that needs to be shared?

When are you going to share it?

Tell, text, or share this with your accountability partner or someone else.

TRANSFORMATION

> Did you recognize any perfectionist tendencies getting in the way of you sharing what needed to be shared?

Do you know yourself better this week than you did last week?

○ Yes ○ No

Did you share this week's Inspiration, Application, or Transformation with someone?

○ Yes ○ No

If not, do it now.

Did you complete your goal?

○ Yes ○ No

---

[1] Antony, M.M., Purdon, K. L., Huta, R. P., and Swinson, L. M. "Perfectionism, Fear of Failure, and Affective Responses to Success and Failure: The Central Role of Fear of Experiencing Shame and Embarrassment," *Journal of Social and Clinical Psychology* (1998)

WEEK 7

IF YOU LOOK FOR THE GOOD, YOU FIND IT. IF YOU LOOK FOR THE BAD, WELL, YOU'LL FIND IT. WHICH ONE ARE YOU LOOKING FOR?

JON GORDON

INSPIRATION

A study conducted by Lord, Ross, and Lepper on biased assimilation and attitude polarization found that when presented with mixed evidence on a controversial topic (in this case, the death penalty's effectiveness as a crime deterrent), participants became more entrenched in their existing views. This study showcased how individuals assimilated evidence in a biased manner, favoring what aligned with their preconceived notions.[1]

Surprised? Probably not. We all do it.

Confirmation bias. It's our brain's crafty little trick to cherry-pick information that confirms our existing beliefs or ideas. We do this with politics, religion, and the people in our lives. Convinced your friend is always late? You bet your brain will spotlight all those instances reinforcing this belief, conveniently turning a blind eye to the times he or she was punctual. The problem with this mindset is that it obstructs the richness of reality. Your outlook on life can shape your experiences and influence your journey. A deliberate quest for goodness is the thing that builds resilience and growth.

Conversely, a pessimistic focus can strangle your potential. It's up to you to decide which perspective you choose to adopt. Strive to embrace the positive, unlocking opportunities for learning and meaningful impact.

WEEK 8

FEELINGS ARE SOMETHING YOU HAVE; NOT SOMETHING YOU ARE.

SHANNON L. ALDER

INSPIRATION

If you don't like how you're currently feeling, this exercise will help. We're going to explore the thoughts that are firing off those pesky emotions. Why? Because they're critical to reclaiming control of your narrative.

Here's how it works: your thoughts ignite your feelings, which in turn fuel your actions. Those actions? They're the bricks and mortar building up your reality.

Years ago, I was feeling extremely frustrated at my inability to drum up business for a specific audience and service I had created. I kept running into walls. Once I analyzed my frustrated feelings, I realized my frustration was more about my own thoughts than the service itself. My thoughts of, "No one wants this," or, "Well, that was a waste of a year" led me down the path of hopelessness. That hopelessness kept me from promoting the service like I should have. No wonder it didn't succeed.

By shaping your thoughts, you can also reshape your reality. It's like taking a master class in self-transformation, and it starts right in the workshop of your own mind. Every thought you entertain, every idea you roll around in your head, is a choice you're making. And these choices sculpt you, shaping you into the person you will become.

APPLICATION

What thought am I having about this person/situation?

Why am I choosing to think this?

How is that thought making me feel?

How do I want to feel?

What new thought would be associated with that feeling?

When will you practice this new way of thinking?

Tell, text, or share this with your accountability partner or someone else.

TRANSFORMATION

> What tendencies caused you to slip back to the negative thought or feeling?

Do you know yourself better this week than you did last week?

○ Yes ○ No

Did you share this week's Inspiration, Application, or Transformation with someone?

○ Yes ○ No

If not, do it now.

Did you complete your goal?

○ Yes ○ No

WEEK 9

THE PERSON WHO TRIGGERS YOU THE MOST CAN BE YOUR GREATEST TEACHER.

INSPIRATION

Ever cross paths with someone who just knows how to hit all the wrong buttons, who seems to navigate the maze of your patience with a touch of annoying expertise? These are not necessarily bad people, but guides in disguise, showing you the areas of yourself that may need a little work.

By shifting your lens to view these encounters as opportunities for learning, you can uncover the hidden gold behind your actions. These interactions can, indeed, be your launchpad for self-discovery.

So, instead of bracing for impact, welcome these moments. By embracing the lessons tucked away in these challenging exchanges, you can fuel your personal and professional evolution, building a more resilient and adaptable mindset. Remember, every obstacle on the trail can be a stepping stone toward growth if you choose to see it that way.

APPLICATION

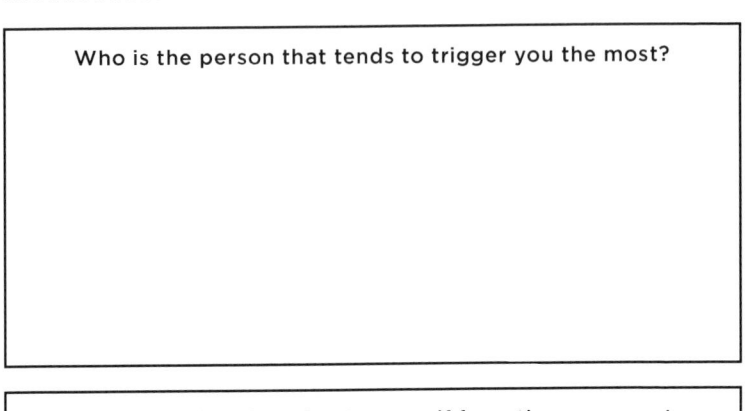

Who is the person that tends to trigger you the most?

What are you learning about yourself from these encounters that can benefit you in your life?

What are you going to do this week to be more intentional about letting these encounters move you forward rather than hold you back?

Tell, text, or share this with your accountability partner or someone else.

TRANSFORMATION

> What tendencies did you need to put back in check so you could make progress?

Do you know yourself better this week than you did last week?

○ Yes ○ No

Did you share this week's Inspiration, Application, or Transformation with someone?

○ Yes ○ No

If not, do it now.

Did you complete your goal?

○ Yes ○ No

WEEK 10

VICTIMS ALWAYS NEED A VILLAIN.

INSPIRATION

The victim mentality is ripe with defensiveness.
Victims want to hide.
Victims tend to complain a lot.
Victims have a negative mentality.
Victims will take things from the past and use them to justify their behavior now.

Have you met someone like this? Or have you perhaps glimpsed shades of this within yourself? Falling prey to a victim mentality can cripple your capacity to grow and thrive. It keeps your lens zoomed in on the supposed injustices tossed your way, instead of empowering you to rise above them.

People with a victim mentality feel as though bad things keep happening to them or the world is against them.

There are three core beliefs underlying the victim mentality:

1. Bad things just happen to me, no matter what I do.
2. Bad things are other people's fault, not mine.
3. I can't change what happens, so there's no point in trying.

This type of thinking tends to come from a sense of not feeling in control. Turning your thoughts from things you can't control to things you can control should be your first step.

You need to break free from these shackles of victimhood and plant the seeds of proactivity and resilience in your mind. This is the true essence of empowerment. It's about intentionally nurturing your inner growth and treating your mental and emotional health with care. As you do this, you will begin to see the opportunities for growth and potential that lie within you.

APPLICATION

When was the last time you felt like a "victim" of someone else's words or actions?

What were the consequences of having a victim mentality?

Make a list of things you can control and things you can't control. Note how much time you may be spending thinking about the things you can't control.

> When are you going to take action on one item from the "things I can control" list?

Tell, text, or share this with your accountability partner or someone else.

TRANSFORMATION

> What tendencies often lead you to having a victim mentality?

Do you know yourself better this week than you did last week?

○ Yes ○ No

Did you share this week's Inspiration, Application, or Transformation with someone?

○ Yes ○ No

If not, do it now.

Did you complete your goal?

○ Yes ○ No

WEEK 11

LEADERS WHO DON'T LISTEN WILL EVENTUALLY BE SURROUNDED BY PEOPLE WHO HAVE NOTHING TO SAY.

ANDY STANLEY

INSPIRATION

In the book, *Are You Really Listening?*, Paul J. Donoghue and Mary E. Siegel found that when leaders actively listened, team cohesion and job satisfaction increased by over 50%.[1]

When leaders choose not to listen, they inadvertently undermine the foundation of trust and collaboration that fuels progress. Only 51% of employees think their leaders are great at listening to them.[2] As a result, these leaders may find themselves surrounded by individuals who no longer feel inspired to share their ideas, ultimately hindering the collective potential for growth and success.

Embracing the power of empathetic listening not only strengthens the relationships between leaders and their teams but also enables the exploration of diverse perspectives, fostering a culture of innovation and mutual respect. Through the act of listening, leaders wield the key to awakening the unbounded potential within their group, ascending in unity, and arriving at the peak of lasting influence.

APPLICATION

> Who is someone in your life you feel doesn't listen to what others have to say?

> How is that person perceived by you or others?

> What's one thing you're going to do to listen more to the people around you?

> When are you going to take action?

Tell, text, or share this with your accountability partner or someone else.

TRANSFORMATION

> What tendencies prevent you from being someone who listens to others?

Do you know yourself better this week than you did last week?

○ Yes   ○ No

Did you share this week's Inspiration, Application, or Transformation with someone?

○ Yes   ○ No

If not, do it now.

Did you complete your goal?

○ Yes   ○ No

---

[1]Donoghue, P.J., and Siegel, M.E. *Are You Really Listening?: Keys to Successful Communication.* Sorin Books, 2005.

[2]"Listening | Global Culture Report" O.C. Tanner, www.octanner.com/global-culture-report/2020-listening. Accessed 6 Nov. 2023.

WEEK 12

ANGER IS A GREAT STARTER BUT A HORRIBLE FINISHER.

INSPIRATION

Anger, like an unexpected storm on a mountain climb, can obscure your trail, disrupt your rhythm, and even start avalanches. It can blur your judgment, fracture team unity, and undermine the crucial trust that forms when you're hanging over the edge of life or work.

The key to all of this is the map to show you where to go.

Studies show that if you don't have a clear plan, feeling angry makes you give up faster and thus, not reach your goals. But, when you know where you are going and you have a plan for when the storm commences, feelings of anger don't really affect your success.[1]

Anger with no plan is just anger. However, anger, when harnessed correctly, can fuel your climb. It's not about suppressing anger, but rather learning to redirect its raw energy into more productive emotions and actions. By converting anger into resolve and understanding, you foster an environment of empathy and collaboration, laying down a safer, clearer path.

This journey isn't about evading the storm but learning to climb amidst any weather. By mastering your own emotional landscape, you carve out a path that inspires others to follow.

APPLICATION

> **When faced with anger, how can you use it to create a clear plan and continue your climb, rather than letting it deter you?**
> *Think of this in terms of action you can take. Let anger be the motivation to get you started.*

> When you feel angry this week, follow the steps you've outlined above.

Tell, text, or share this with your accountability partner or someone else.

TRANSFORMATION

What tendencies prevented you from following your plan?

Do you know yourself better this week than you did last week?

○ Yes ○ No

Did you share this week's Inspiration, Application, or Transformation with someone?

○ Yes ○ No

If not, do it now.

Did you complete your goal?

○ Yes ○ No

---

[1]Schmitt, A., Gielnik, M.M. & Seibel, S. "When and how does anger during goal pursuit relate to goal achievement? The roles of persistence and action planning." Motiv Emot **43**, 205–217 (2019). https://doi.org/10.1007/s11031-018-9720-4

CHECK-IN

IT'S CHECK-IN TIME!

It's check-in time!

Be honest in your evaluation. You should see some progress by now if you've been doing the work. Rate yourself here, then go back and compare this to your previous numbers.

If your score has improved, give yourself a high-five and keep going!

If you've seen a dip, give yourself a high-five and keep going!

Wait, what? Why would you do that, you ask? Because as you become more and more self-aware, you'll begin to navigate life and relationships better than ever before. In fact, this "dip" may not be things getting worse at all, but rather evidence that you are becoming more aware of who you are and some of your challenges. It's up to you to decide what the data is telling you.

I also want to celebrate you for making it this far. You've been doing the work. You're further up the mountain than when you started, and maybe you've struggled along the way. Each struggle is a lesson and an opportunity for growth.

Plus, how often do you actually high-five yourself?

THE TWO SIDES OF LEADERSHIP

Rate yourself from 1-10, with 1 being the lowest and 10 being the highest:

RATE HOW WELL YOU'RE PERSONALLY PERFORMING:

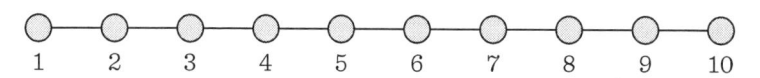

1 — 2 — 3 — 4 — 5 — 6 — 7 — 8 — 9 — 10

RATE HOW WELL YOU ARE LEADING OTHER PERFORMERS:

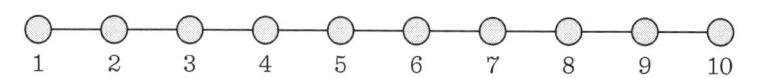

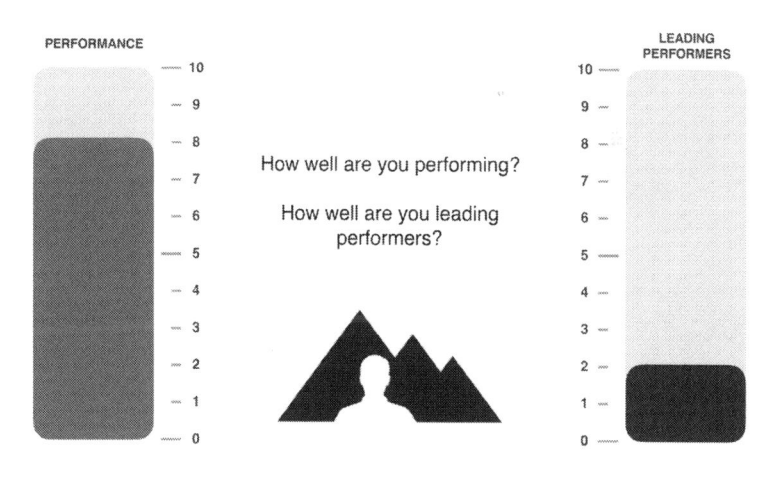

1 — 2 — 3 — 4 — 5 — 6 — 7 — 8 — 9 — 10

PERFORMANCE

LEADING PERFORMERS

How well are you performing?

How well are you leading performers?

GiANT

© Pub House

KNOW YOURSELF

SUPPORT AND CHALLENGE

How have you been showing up lately? Using the graphic below, plot yourself on the matrix just like you did when you created your baseline. Make a dot for each circle of influence (self, family, team, organization, community). You should have at least five dots at the end of the exercise. Go back and compare this round to your baseline analysis when you started this journey. Have any of the dots moved from the protect, abdicate, or dominate quadrants to the liberate quadrant?

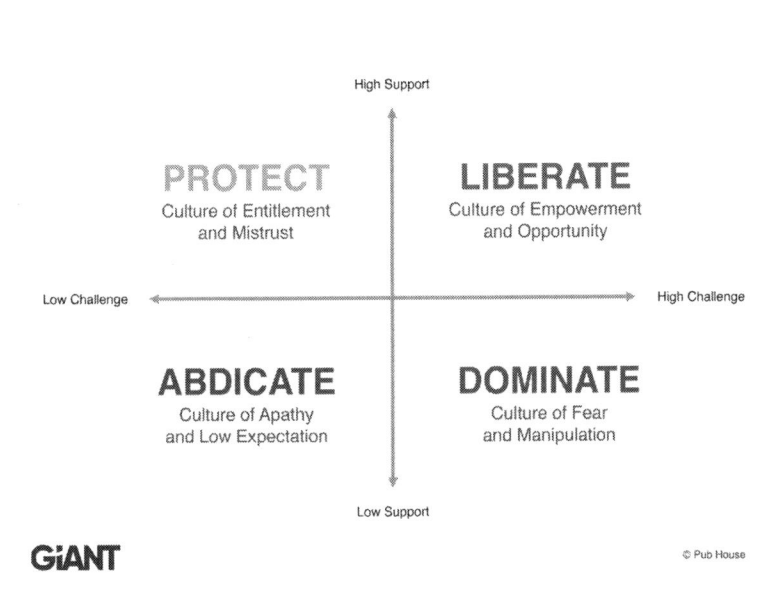

	High Support	
PROTECT Culture of Entitlement and Mistrust		**LIBERATE** Culture of Empowerment and Opportunity
Low Challenge ←———————————————————→ High Challenge		
ABDICATE Culture of Apathy and Low Expectation		**DOMINATE** Culture of Fear and Manipulation
	Low Support	

GiANT © Pub House

KNOW, LOVE, LEAD

Rate yourself 1-10 on how well you know yourself, how much you love yourself, and how well you lead yourself, with 1 being the lowest score and 10 being the highest.

KNOW:

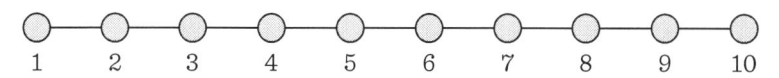

1 — 2 — 3 — 4 — 5 — 6 — 7 — 8 — 9 — 10

LOVE:

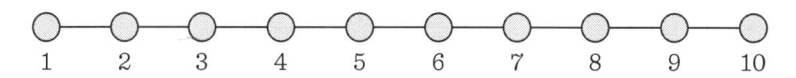

1 — 2 — 3 — 4 — 5 — 6 — 7 — 8 — 9 — 10

LEAD:

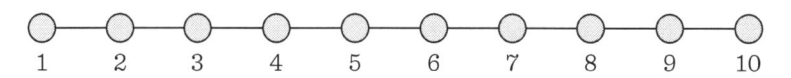

1 — 2 — 3 — 4 — 5 — 6 — 7 — 8 — 9 — 10

THESE ARE A FEW TOOLS OUT OF 60+ TOTAL TOOLS I USE TO COACH MY CLIENTS. GAIN ACCESS TO ALL OF THEM AT WWW.SKOTWALDRON.COM/TOOLS.

> Where were you doing better or worse based on your initial evaluation at the beginning of the book?

> What's going well?

> Where are you struggling, and what can you do to improve this?

> What's your biggest win of the first 12 weeks?

> Who are you going to share that with, and when?

WEEK 13

EVERY TIME I REPEAT A FEARFUL OR DEFEATIST THOUGHT, I STRENGTHEN THE CONNECTIONS THAT MAKE IT EASIER TO HAVE THAT THOUGHT AGAIN.

DR. HENRY EMMONS

INSPIRATION

You tend to get a lot better at the things you practice. Continually indulging in fear or defeatist thinking only serves to strengthen the neural pathways that reinforce these thoughts, making it increasingly difficult to break free from their grip.

It's like a song you can't get out of your head but way less fun. Some brainy folks call this 'repetitive negative thinking,' which is basically the evil twin of both rumination (overthinking past mistakes) and worry (stressing about the future). A study with over 600 college students showed that this kind of thinking links strongly to both depressive and anxious feelings. And that's not all. This negative thinking also ties into random, unwelcome thoughts popping into our minds, making it harder for us to be present and mindful.[1]

To overcome this mental trap, you must recognize these patterns and consciously replace them with more empowering thoughts, enabling you to cultivate a mindset of optimism, resilience, and determination that propels you forward on your journey of success and fulfillment.

APPLICATION

> Which fearful or defeatist thought do you regularly find yourself thinking?

> What's a different thought you can try out instead?
> *Don't make it a lie. Your brain is too smart for that.*
> *The new thought must be believable.*

> When are you going to practice this thought?

Tell, text, or share this with your accountability partner or someone else.

TRANSFORMATION

> Which of your tendencies increases the likelihood of having a fearful or defeatist thought?

Do you know yourself better this week than you did last week?

○ Yes   ○ No

Did you share this week's Inspiration, Application, or Transformation with someone?

○ Yes   ○ No

If not, do it now.

Did you complete your goal?

○ Yes   ○ No

---

[1]Gustavson, Daniel E, et al. "Evidence for Transdiagnostic Repetitive Negative Thinking and Its Association with Rumination, Worry, and Depression and Anxiety Symptoms: A Commonality Analysis." *Collabra. Psychology,* U.S. National Library of Medicine, 2018, www.ncbi.nlm.nih.gov/pmc/articles/PMC6370308/#:~:text=In%20 these%20studies%2C%20repetitive%20negative,symptoms%20in%20university%20 students%20up.

WEEK 14

IF YOU ARE COMFORTABLE ALL THE TIME, THEN YOU'RE PROBABLY MEDIOCRE. THE COMFORT ZONE IS LINED WITH DEFENSIVENESS AND EXCUSES FOR WHY YOU SHOULD STAY THERE.

INSPIRATION

Let's face it - we all have areas in life where we're just average. But what about the skills that truly make a difference - effective communication, self-leadership, influence, empowering others? Are you okay with being just average in these domains?

Settling into the comfort of a known quantity can often lead to mediocrity. It hinders the exploration of new ideas and experiences, keeping you wrapped in a cocoon of complacency filled with limiting beliefs that hold you back.

Dr. Russo-Netzer and her collaborator Geoffrey L. Cohen designed a novel intervention called a 'behavioral stretch intervention' that encouraged people to take up activities that were previously outside of their comfort zone.[1]

The study found that engaging in activities at the edge of one's comfort zone boosted the life satisfaction of people who started out with relatively low life satisfaction.

To truly shine, you must dare to step outside of your comfort zone and into the realm of the unknown. It's here that you expand your horizons and foster a mindset of continuous learning and growth. Only then can you evolve from being just average to truly exceptional.

APPLICATION

In which areas of your life have you been confining yourself to your comfort zone? What are you going to do to step outside of that zone?

When are you going to take action?

Tell, text, or share this with your accountability partner or someone else.

TRANSFORMATION

....

> What tendencies made you want to step back into your comfort zone?

Do you know yourself better this week than you did last week?

○ Yes ○ No

Did you share this week's Inspiration, Application, or Transformation with someone?

○ Yes ○ No

If not, do it now.

Did you complete your goal?

○ Yes ○ No

[1] Russo-Netzer, Pninit & Cohen, Geoffrey. (2022). 'If you're uncomfortable, go outside your comfort zone': A novel behavioral 'stretch' intervention supports the well-being of unhappy people. *The Journal of Positive Psychology*. 18. 1-17. 10.1080/17439760.2022.2036794.

WEEK 15

PAIN AND VULNERABILITY PRECEDE BREAKTHROUGHS.

BRENÉ BROWN

INSPIRATION

Sometimes, it is the torrential downpour that enables you to appreciate the warmth of sunlight. Pain and vulnerability are often precursors to personal breakthroughs, as they expose your weaknesses and challenge you to rise above them.

Anna Bruk and her team over at the University of Mannheim, taking a page out of Brené Brown's playbook, dug deep into the world of vulnerability. And guess what they found? This quirky thing called the "beautiful mess effect." When people imagined themselves in those vulnerable moments—like admitting a royal screw-up at work—they felt they'd come off looking weak. But when flipping the script and imagining someone else doing the same thing, participants saw it as not only brave but positive and admirable.[1]

It seems we're harder on ourselves than on others when it comes to showing our true feelings and emotions.

By facing these difficult moments with courage and determination, you unlock new levels of personal growth and development, fortifying your resilience and paving the way for future success. Embracing these moments of vulnerability allows you to transcend your limitations, fostering a mindset of continuous growth and transformation that drives you to achieve your full potential.

APPLICATION

Let's focus on the vulnerability part here.
I want you to finish this statement:

If you really knew me, you'd know that I _____.

Repeat it five times, and each time become more vulnerable.

Tell, text, or share this with your accountability partner or someone else.

TRANSFORMATION

> What tendencies caused you to want to hold back from becoming more vulnerable?

Do you know yourself better this week than you did last week?

○ Yes ○ No

Did you share this week's Inspiration, Application, or Transformation with someone?

○ Yes ○ No

If not, do it now.

Did you complete your goal?

○ Yes ○ No

> How did you feel after completing this exercise and sharing it with someone?

[1] Bruk, A., Scholl, S. G., & Bless, H. (2018). "Beautiful mess effect: Self-other differences in evaluation of showing vulnerability." Journal of Personality and Social Psychology, 115(2), 192–205. https://doi.org/10.1037/pspa0000120

WEEK 16

ALWAYS LONGING FOR MORE IS A FEAR OF NOT HAVING ENOUGH.

INSPIRATION

A constant desire for more may be a reflection of your deeply-seated insecurities about scarcity. It underscores the relationship between desire and fear, indicating that your pursuit for more often stems from an underlying fear of inadequacy or insufficiency. This way of thinking can trigger an unending spiral of dissatisfaction, where scarcity overshadows your ability to appreciate what's already in your hands.

I've been there all too often. I've worked for years on my mindset around money and entrepreneurship. Not having enough clients, not having enough money, not having enough time, not having enough people to get things done, etc. The funny thing about all of this is that I've usually had "enough." It hasn't always been comfortable, and at times it was pretty scary. But I've always been able to provide what I needed for my family and business to survive.

Having a "scarcity mindset" changes how your brain works when making choices. Specifically, people with a scarcity mindset show more activity in the part of the brain that deals with valuing things (the orbitofrontal cortex) and less activity in the part that helps with making goal-oriented choices (the dorsolateral prefrontal cortex). Interestingly, a study showed that these brain activity changes were most noticeable in people who had recently experienced abundance before switching to a scarcity mindset. So, in simpler terms, thinking you don't have enough can mess with your brain's decision-making skills, especially if you're used to having enough.[1]

This serves as a reminder to cultivate gratitude and contentment in your life, acknowledging and appreciating your present circumstances instead of constantly yearning for more.

It should prompt you to reframe your perspective, shifting from scarcity to abundance and savoring the beauty in your current situation. The key is not in having more but in recognizing that you already have enough and cultivating an attitude of appreciation.

APPLICATION

Where do you feel scarcity in your life?

Where do you think that comes from?

This week, write down five things every morning you're grateful for.

Tell, text, or share this with your accountability partner or someone else.

TRANSFORMATION

....

> How did you feel when writing the gratitude items vs. thinking about the scarcity items?

Do you know yourself better this week than you did last week?

○ Yes   ○ No

Did you share this week's Inspiration, Application, or Transformation with someone?

○ Yes   ○ No

If not, do it now.

Did you complete your goal?

○ Yes   ○ No

> How did you feel after completing this exercise and sharing it with someone?

[1]Huijsmans, Inge. "A Scarcity Mindset Alters Neural Processing Underlying Consumer ... - PNASInge Huijsmans." *PNAS Logo,* PSYCHOLOGICAL AND COGNITIVE SCIENCES, 23 May 2019, www.pnas.org/doi/10.1073/pnas.1818572116.

WEEK 17

NOTHING TO FEAR.
NOTHING TO HIDE.
NOTHING TO PROVE.

JEREMIE KUBICEK

INSPIRATION

A mindset free from fear, concealment, and the need to prove oneself can be incredibly liberating, fostering an environment of open communication, authenticity, and personal growth. By embracing this attitude, you can focus on meaningful self-improvement, ultimately contributing to a more productive atmosphere where everyone can thrive. Fear, hiding, and proving oneself in unhealthy ways often lead to losing the very thing we're trying to protect.

Ironically, fear-based behaviors—attempts to conceal your true self or constantly prove your worth—often jeopardize the very thing you're striving to protect. Such attitudes can lead you further from your sought-after sense of security and acceptance.

Liberate yourself from these self-imposed chains and embrace the empowering practices of openness, authenticity, and healthy self-improvement.

APPLICATION

What are you afraid of losing?

What are you trying to hide?

What are you trying to prove?

Choose one action you can take this week to improve one of the three areas highlighted above.

Tell, text, or share this with your accountability partner or someone else.

TRANSFORMATION

> Were you afraid of losing something this past week?
> Trying to hide something? Or, trying to prove something?

Do you know yourself better this week than you did last week?

○ Yes   ○ No

Did you share this week's Inspiration, Application, or Transformation with someone?

○ Yes   ○ No

If not, do it now.

Did you complete your goal?

○ Yes   ○ No

HEAR MORE INSIGHTS FROM JEREMIE AND STEVE BY VISITING WWW.SKOTWALDRON.COM/FOUNDERS.

UNLOCKING THE COMMUNICATION CODE WITH JEREMIE KUBICEK AND STEVE COCKRAM

with guest
JEREMIE KUBICEK
CO-FOUNDER
GIANT

with guest
STEVE COCKRAM
CO-FOUNDER
GIANT

UNLOCKED

WEEK 18

ARE YOU MAKING A LIVING OR MAKING AN IMPACT?

INSPIRATION

Two peaks lie before you. One represents a life of financial stability; the other embodies a life of social impact. One is all about the 9-to-5 grind, secure but perhaps a bit monotonous. It promises a straightforward climb but leaves you questioning the legacy you're creating. The other is rugged but rewarding, fraught with challenges yet rich in purpose.

Having to choose between these two options can stir up some internal dilemmas. The orbitofrontal cortex, the part of your brain that places value on things, might be buzzing with activity as you ponder financial benefits and job security. Meanwhile, your dorsolateral prefrontal cortex, the part involved in long-term decision-making, may be quieter, especially if you've tasted financial comfort before and are now facing the ethical dilemma of impact versus income. Just like thinking you don't have enough can mess with your brain, so can this decision.

Rather than agonizing over the choice, why not find a middle ground? It's not just about grinding day in and day out to earn a living; it's also about what sort of impact you're leaving in your wake. Aim for a summit that offers not just a panoramic view of your personal achievements, but also a legacy that impacts others. This journey is about appreciating what you have, acknowledging your potential to influence, and understanding that making a living and making an impact are not mutually exclusive.

At the end of it all, when you look back, you won't just see a life spent accumulating comforts. You'll see a life that mattered, a life that balanced the scales of personal gain and impact.

APPLICATION

> What are the contributions you're making?

> What's the impact you're having on others because of those contributions?

> Create a sentence using this framework:
> I (contribution from above) so that (impact from above).

Tell, text, or share this with your accountability partner or someone else.

TRANSFORMATION

Do you know yourself better this week than you did last week?

◯ Yes ◯ No

Read your statement again. Did you see evidence of it this past week?

◯ Yes ◯ No

Did you share this week's Inspiration, Application, or Transformation with someone?

◯ Yes ◯ No

If not, do it now.

Did you complete your goal?

◯ Yes ◯ No

WEEK 19

SECURE, CONFIDENT, AND HUMBLE

JEREMIE KUBICEK

INSPIRATION

Have you ever been led by someone who was insecure, arrogant, or prideful?

My guess is it didn't go well.

My guess is you don't have fond memories of working with that person.

My guess is they didn't have a positive influence on you.

A secure person doesn't waste time second-guessing every move or seeking constant validation. They make decisions based on well-grounded self-assurance, not on a shaky foundation of doubt. Confidence lets you take calculated risks, push the boundaries, and grow. But what balances it all out is humility. It reminds you that you're part of a larger universe, that everyone has something valuable to contribute, and that listening can sometimes be more powerful than speaking. It means you're teachable

APPLICATION

> Do you need to work on becoming more secure, confident, or humble?

> Specify one of those three concepts and state how you plan to improve in that area this week.

Tell, text, or share this with your accountability partner or someone else.

TRANSFORMATION

> Did you notice a drop in resistance from practicing being more secure, confident, or humble?

Do you know yourself better this week than you did last week?

○ Yes ○ No

Did you share this week's Inspiration, Application, or Transformation with someone?

○ Yes ○ No

If not, do it now.

Did you complete your goal?

○ Yes ○ No

HEAR MORE INSIGHTS FROM JEREMIE AND STEVE BY VISITING WWW.SKOTWALDRON.COM/FOUNDERS.

Part Two

LOVE YOURSELF

WEEK 20

TO DEEPEN YOUR LOVE AND ACCEPTANCE OF ANOTHER, FIRST, DEVELOP LOVE AND ACCEPTANCE FOR YOURSELF.

INSPIRATION

Imagine your life as a mountainous terrain. At the base, you find many people stuck, afraid to climb, fearing the steep paths and the unknown pitfalls. They've never invested in the emotional "gear" needed for the ascent: the ropes of self-compassion, the hooks of self-worth, or the boots of self-respect. They can't possibly help others ascend if they've never made the climb themselves.

Then there are those who've taken the first steps, their packs filled with essentials for the journey: acknowledgment of their own worth, forgiveness for their own faults, and unconditional love for themselves. With each step upwards, their packs become lighter as they unload insecurities, self-doubt, and past troubles. The higher they climb, the more expansive the view becomes. From this elevated vantage point, they can more easily reach down and offer a helping hand to others who are also making their way up the mountain. They guide them not out of a need for validation but from a genuine desire to share the breathtaking view that can only be seen after a challenging climb.

But remember, this mountain has no summit. The journey is ongoing, a perpetual cycle of self-discovery and love that enriches your ability to help others on their own climbs. The terrain might get rough; you might encounter storms of self-doubt or foggy patches of confusion. That's okay. With your well-stocked pack of self-awesomeness, you're well-equipped for the journey. And as you continue to ascend, you'll find that you're not just climbing alone; you're part of a community, all of you intertwined in this intricate dance of giving and receiving love. And the most beautiful part? The higher you climb, the more love you have to give, elevating not just yourself but everyone fortunate enough to cross paths with you on this lifelong ascent.

APPLICATION

> What's one thing you need to accept more about who you are?

> What are you going to do this week to appreciate yourself more?

Tell, text, or share this with your accountability partner or someone else.

TRANSFORMATION

> How are you feeling now that you've been through this exercise?

Do you know yourself better this week than you did last week?

◯ Yes ◯ No

Did you share this week's Inspiration, Application, or Transformation with someone?

◯ Yes ◯ No

If not, do it now.

Did you complete your goal?

◯ Yes ◯ No

WEEK 21

"I'LL BE HAPPY WHEN…"
VS.
"I'LL BE HAPPY WHILE…"

INSPIRATION

Always longing for something that may or may not become a reality is a recipe for misery. For years, I gauged my own progress by juxtaposing myself against "successful" friends and family, utilizing their accomplishments as a yardstick for my own fulfillment. Here's the problem – despite reaching some of these milestones, there was always another peak to scale. The goals I had strived for but hadn't yet reached? They persist because they were not genuinely mine. They belonged to others.

Dr. Peart says in her book, *FutureProofed: How To Navigate Disruptive Change, Find Calm in Chaos, and Succeed in Work & Life* that there are plenty of ways to treat "I'll be happy when" syndrome.[1]

"To cure 'I'll be happy when' syndrome, we must start seeing success as a lifestyle, not a destination, so that you can finally be happy *now*—wherever you are in life."

I hold the reins to my happiness, and I can declare contentment at any point on my journey. So, I choose now. I choose to embrace happiness, here in this moment, not as a future goal but as a present reality. And so should you.

APPLICATION

> **When are you going to choose to be happy in your current circumstances?**

> **If you can't do it right now, why not?**
> *Make a plan for how/when you will be able to embrace this mindset.*

Tell, text, or share this with your accountability partner or someone else.

TRANSFORMATION

> Was it hard to "be happy while"? Did you find yourself still saying you'll "be happy when"?

Do you know yourself better this week than you did last week?

◯ Yes ◯ No

Did you share this week's Inspiration, Application, or Transformation with someone?

◯ Yes ◯ No

If not, do it now.

Did you complete your goal?

◯ Yes ◯ No

---

[1] Peart, N. *Future Proofed: The New Rules of Success in Work & Life for Our Modern World.* Scrivener Books, 2019.

WEEK 22

FREE TO BE ME.

INSPIRATION

Imagine, just for a moment, that the world has handed you a golden ticket: permission to be unapologetically you. No strings attached.

What would that be like? Permission from your spouse, from your kids, from your parents, from your boss, from your colleagues.

That permission would bring peace and liberation. It would reduce your stress about having to speak or act a certain way all the time. No more protecting your insecurities, defending your weaknesses, or tip-toeing around people. Complete freedom to ask difficult questions, to be sensitive, to be strong-willed, to be an introvert or extrovert, to want control, or to be that person who waves to everyone they see without fear of judgment.

The freedom to own it and be it, whatever "it" is for you.

What would that be like? It would be liberating.

Here's the thing. You don't need their permission. You only need your own. Give yourself permission to be your unapologetically best self.

APPLICATION

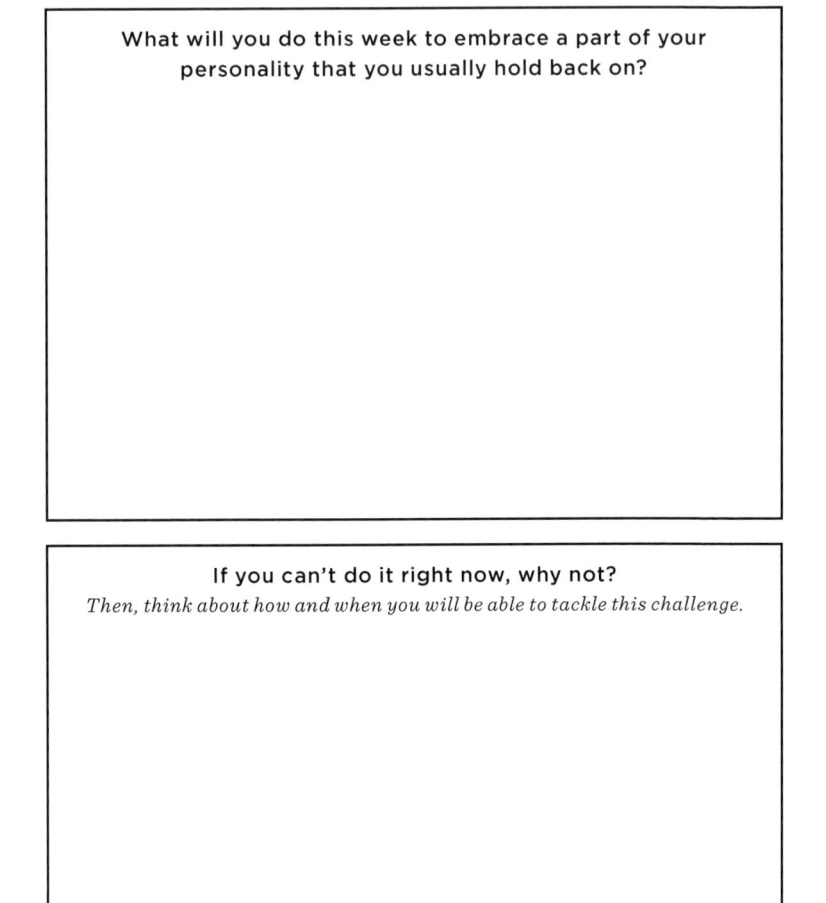

> **What will you do this week to embrace a part of your personality that you usually hold back on?**

> **If you can't do it right now, why not?**
> *Then, think about how and when you will be able to tackle this challenge.*

Tell, text, or share this with your accountability partner or someone else.

TRANSFORMATION

> Do you feel more free to be you and more authentic?

Do you know yourself better this week than you did last week?

○ Yes ○ No

Did you share this week's Inspiration, Application, or Transformation with someone?

○ Yes ○ No

If not, do it now.

Did you complete your goal?

○ Yes ○ No

WEEK 23

IF SOMEONE SEES SOMETHING IN YOU, MAYBE IT'S TIME YOU START SEEING IT, TOO.

INSPIRATION

Imagine I hand you a gift wrapped with care, and as you reach out to take it, you hesitate, push it back toward me, and start downplaying your abilities, explaining why you shouldn't receive it. Kinda feels off, doesn't it?

When I compliment you, the last thing I want to do is fight to convince you that what I've just said is true. I get it. You're humble. You don't want to be in the limelight or to seem arrogant. But I'm complimenting you for a reason. It's because I see something in you. You have impacted me so profoundly that I felt compelled to vocalize it. That's significant. Please don't deny me the joy of expressing my appreciation, and don't deprive yourself of the praise you deserve.

Christopher Littlefield found that even though a whopping 88% of people link feeling valued to getting recognized, nearly 70% also said it makes them feel uncomfortable or embarrassed.[1] And it's not just on the receiving end; a 2020 study in the "Personality and Social Science Bulletin" showed that giving compliments also makes people feel anxious.[2]

So next time, just say "thank you." Allow yourself to bask in that warm fuzzy feeling, and let me have my moment, too. It's a win-win, my friend.

APPLICATION

Do you tend to deflect compliments? If so, why might this be?

To every compliment you receive this week, respond with, "Thank you." That's it.

Tell, text, or share this with your accountability partner or someone else.

TRANSFORMATION

> How did it feel just saying, "thank you"? Was it hard? Easy?

Do you know yourself better this week than you did last week?

◯ Yes   ◯ No

Did you share this week's Inspiration, Application, or Transformation with someone?

◯ Yes   ◯ No

If not, do it now.

Did you complete your goal?

◯ Yes   ◯ No

---

[1] Littlefield, Christopher. "How to Give and Receive Compliments at Work" 12 Oct. 2019, hbr.org/2019/10/how-to-give-and-receive-compliments-at-work. Accessed 6 Nov. 2023.
[2] Boothby, E. J., & Bohns, V. K. (2021). "Why a Simple Act of Kindness Is Not as Simple as It Seems: Underestimating the Positive Impact of Our Compliments on Others." *Personality and Social Psychology Bulletin*, 47(5), 826-840. https://doi.org/10.1177/0146167220949003

WEEK 24

SELF-CRITICISM MAKES YOU BOTH THE ATTACKER AND THE ATTACKED.

KRISTEN NEFF, PHD AND CHRIS GERMER, PHD

INSPIRATION

Picture this: a mini-you with boxing gloves in a ring, throwing punches. But guess who's on the receiving end? Yep, you again. That's what self-criticism feels like – you're both the boxer and the punching bag. It's like a whirlwind of jabs and uppercuts, but they're all formed of doubts and self-disapproval.

This internal slugfest doesn't do you any good. It shreds your confidence, stalls you in your tracks, and let's not even get started on what it does to your mental well-being.

But wait, what if you switch gears? What if you become your own cheerleader instead of being a relentless critic? There's magic in a little bit of self-compassion. Go easy on yourself. Understand that to err is human.

A study in the OMEGA: Journal of Death and Dying found clear evidence that self-compassion may serve as a vital mechanism of change, underscoring the value of mindfulness- and acceptance-based treatments that foster self-compassion.[1]

Swap those boxing gloves for a cup of tea and have a gentle chat with yourself. Focus on growing and learning. After all, the most epic battles you can win are the ones where you conquer your inner critics and embrace the path to bettering yourself.

APPLICATION

In what areas of your life are you self-critical?

What will you do or say to become more accepting of yourself in the area which is most affecting you?

Tell, text, or share this with your accountability partner or someone else.

TRANSFORMATION

Do you know yourself better this week than you did last week?

◯ Yes   ◯ No

Did you feel better about yourself this week?

◯ Yes   ◯ No

Did you share this week's Inspiration, Application, or Transformation with someone?

◯ Yes   ◯ No

If not, do it now.

Did you complete your goal?

◯ Yes   ◯ No

---

[1]Zhang, Huaiyu & Watson-Singleton, Natalie & Pollard, Sara & Pittman, Delishia & Lamis, Dorian & Fischer, Nicole & Patterson, Bobbi & Kaslow, Nadine. (2017). "Self-Criticism and Depressive Symptoms: Mediating Role of Self-Compassion." *OMEGA - Journal of Death and Dying.* 80. 003022281772960. 10.1177/0030222817729609.

CHECK-IN

IT'S CHECK-IN TIME!

It's that time again!

The top rule? Be honest in your evaluation. By this point, you've hopefully created a habit. You may have been super disciplined and done this week after week, or you may have abandoned that whole idea and just created your own schedule. Whatever works for you. I just want you to be consistent!

Rate yourself here, then go back and compare these scores to your previous numbers.

Did your score improve? Give yourself a high-five!

Did you see a dip? Why? Give yourself a high-five for that as well.

Keep going. The trek isn't over. Spoiler alert: it never will be. It's a continuous climb of self-improvement that will be more and more liberating each day.

THE TWO SIDES OF LEADERSHIP

Rate yourself from 1-10, with 1 being the lowest and 10 being the highest:

RATE HOW WELL YOU'RE PERSONALLY PERFORMING:

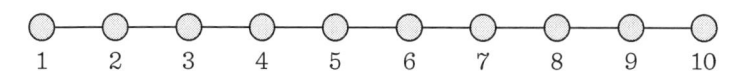

1 2 3 4 5 6 7 8 9 10

RATE HOW WELL YOU ARE LEADING OTHERS:

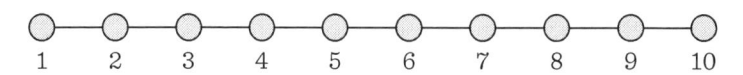

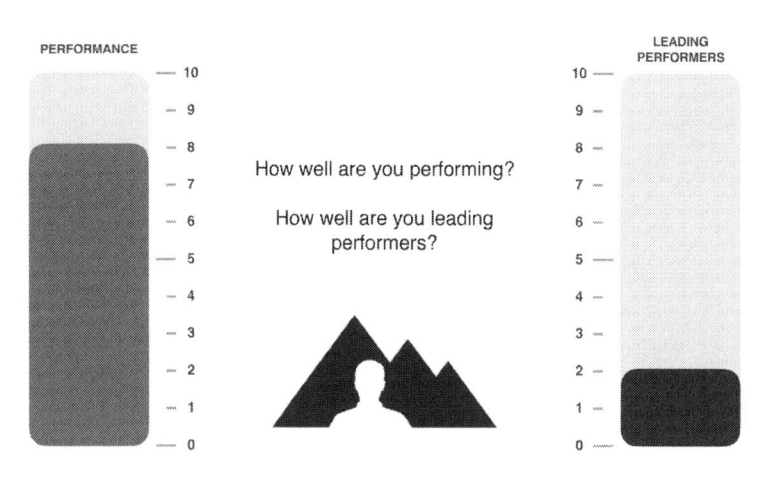

1 2 3 4 5 6 7 8 9 10

PERFORMANCE

LEADING PERFORMERS

How well are you performing?

How well are you leading performers?

GiANT

© Pub House

LOVE YOURSELF

SUPPORT AND CHALLENGE

Using the graphic below, plot yourself on the matrix. Make a dot for each circle of influence (self, family, team, organization, community). You should have at least five dots at the end of the exercise. Now, go back and compare.

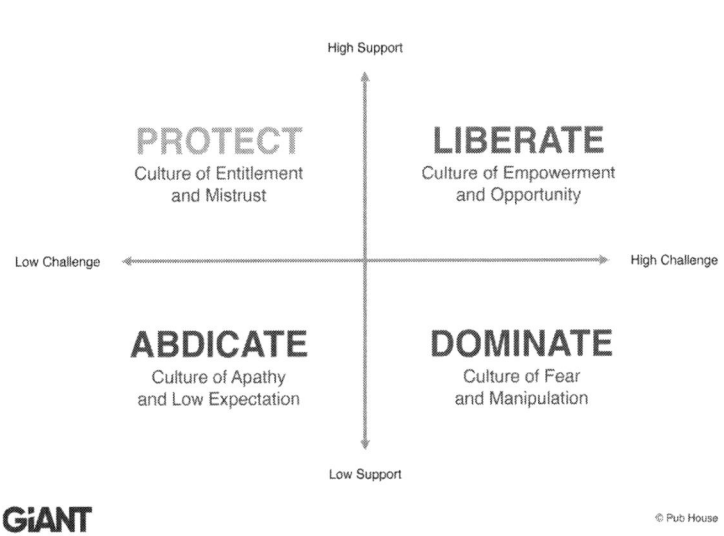

High Support

PROTECT
Culture of Entitlement
and Mistrust

LIBERATE
Culture of Empowerment
and Opportunity

Low Challenge ⟵⟶ High Challenge

ABDICATE
Culture of Apathy
and Low Expectation

DOMINATE
Culture of Fear
and Manipulation

Low Support

GiANT

© Pub House

KNOW, LOVE, LEAD

Rate yourself 1-10 on how well you know yourself, how much you love yourself, and how well you lead yourself, with 1 being the lowest score and 10 being the highest.

KNOW:

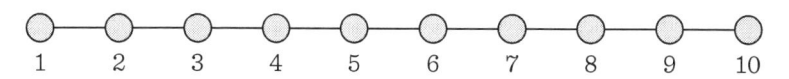

○—○—○—○—○—○—○—○—○—○
1   2   3   4   5   6   7   8   9   10

LOVE:

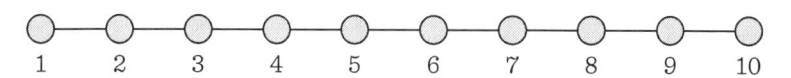

○—○—○—○—○—○—○—○—○—○
1   2   3   4   5   6   7   8   9   10

LEAD:

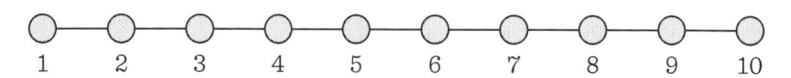

○—○—○—○—○—○—○—○—○—○
1   2   3   4   5   6   7   8   9   10

THESE ARE A FEW TOOLS OUT OF 60+ TOTAL TOOLS I USE TO COACH MY CLIENTS. GAIN ACCESS TO ALL OF THEM AT WWW.SKOTWALDRON.COM/TOOLS.

> Where were you doing better or worse
> than your previous evaluations?

> Look at the last question of each week that asks, "Did you
> complete your goal?" How many have you completed so far?

> What's going well?

> Where are you struggling, and
> what can you do to improve this?

> What's your biggest win of the second 12 weeks?

> Who are you going to share that with, and when?

LOVE YOURSELF

WEEK 25

YESTERDAY TEACHES TODAY, IT DOESN'T DEFINE IT.

JOHN C. MAXWELL

INSPIRATION

Yesterday is like a well-thumbed mountain guidebook with notes in the margins - it's got some wisdom, regrets, and hard-earned lessons. Each page is a stepping stone that led you here, to the now.

It's easy to get caught in the shadow of yesterday's chapters. But don't forget, yesterday gave you some great tools. You're armed with insights, a dash of hindsight, and maybe some newfound resolve.

When you're fully tuned in to the 'now,' you stop playing the spectator of the past. You get to notice details you'd otherwise miss, from the smile of a stranger to the flavor of your favorite ice cream. These opportunities are like hidden gems sprinkled throughout your day; being present lets you spot and snag them.

Let yesterday be the guidebook, tattered and worn, teaching you what it needs to teach you. Let today be the fresh, blank page of wonder, ideas, and opportunity. No matter how messy yesterday was, it doesn't control the direction of today's adventure.

APPLICATION

What's something in the past that you feel is holding you back right now?

Are you willing to let it go? If not, why not?

What is one thing you could do to focus on this current stage of life rather than the past?

Tell, text, or share this with your accountability partner or someone else.

TRANSFORMATION

> I realize things don't just vanish; it'll take time.
> But how did it feel to start letting go of the past?

Do you know yourself better this week than you did last week?

◯ Yes ◯ No

Did you share this week's Inspiration, Application, or Transformation with someone?

◯ Yes ◯ No

If not, do it now.

Did you complete your goal?

◯ Yes ◯ No

WEEK 26

I COULD LIKE ME LATER, OR I COULD LIKE ME RIGHT NOW.

INSPIRATION

Researchers looked at how self-esteem and self-love impact our self-view. They found that generally, people rate themselves higher on positive traits than negative ones. And get this! The higher the self-esteem, the more they pumped up their positives.

Now, on the science side of things, they also looked at brain waves. The brain actually shows different activity when we think about traits that align with our own positive self-view. For people with low self-esteem, their brain activity indicates they take a little longer to process this information.[1]

How you feel about yourself plays a huge role in your behavior and how your brain processes information about you.

We sometimes chase the person we want to be with such ferocity that we forget to love who we are at this very moment.

In my life, I've found the person I wanted to be is that friend of mine with a seemingly nice job, paycheck, house, and boat. The person I wanted to be was that family member who seemed like they had it all together. I wanted to be that family I see traveling all the time.

I've had to really concentrate on being me. On being who I am at this moment. Accepting me, right now, has offered me more mental freedom than any of those other identities I was longing for.

Both versions deserve a high five. Your future self is your vision, your goals, your aspirations. It's the "you" that keeps you on your toes.

Meanwhile, the present "you" is the hiker, trekking up that mountainside. It's the character grinding through the daily quests, celebrating the small wins, and sometimes just finding the strength to get out of bed.

So, how about a compromise? Let's cheer for the person

you're becoming, but let's not wait for the confetti to rain down to start the party. Throw a dash of kindness to the person in the mirror. A blend of appreciation for today's grit and excitement for tomorrow's glory makes a fine recipe for self-acceptance.

APPLICATION

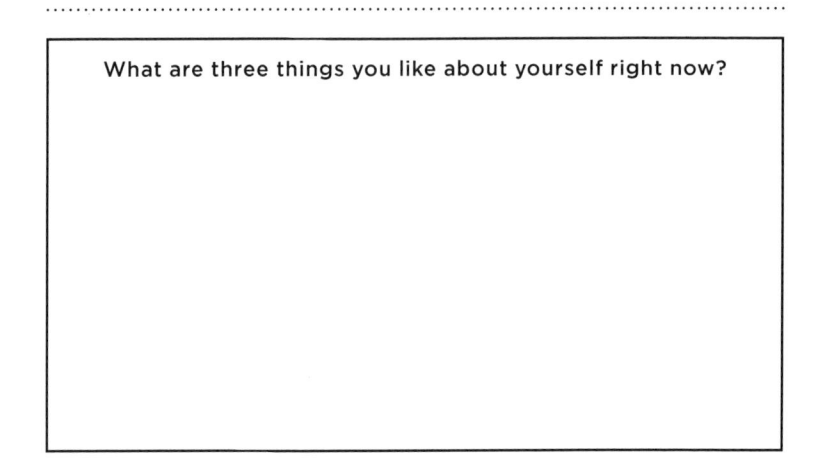

What are three things you like about yourself right now?

How are those things going to help you be the person you want to be in the future?

Tell, text, or share this with your accountability partner or someone else.

TRANSFORMATION

> Write down three more things you like about yourself. How does that feel?

Do you know yourself better this week than you did last week?

◯ Yes ◯ No

Did you share this week's Inspiration, Application, or Transformation with someone?

◯ Yes ◯ No

If not, do it now.

Did you complete your goal?

◯ Yes ◯ No

---

[1] Zhang H, Guan L, Qi M, Yang J. "Self-esteem modulates the time course of self-positivity bias in explicit self-evaluation." *PLoS One*. 2013 Dec 5;8(12):e81169. doi: 10.1371/journal.pone.0081169. PMID: 24339908; PMCID: PMC3855207.

WEEK 27

SNEAKERS ARE CHEAPER THAN KNEES.

JON ACUFF

INSPIRATION

Jon shared this quote on his podcast. He's a runner and would dread buying new shoes because of how expensive they are. So, he'd completely wear out his current running shoes, wanting to get every last mile out of them. One day, his wife said, "Jon, sneakers are cheaper than knees."

Make the investment in long-term gain (keeping your knees), rather than focusing on the short-term pain (the cost of new shoes).

It's referred to as, "hyperbolic discounting" – our inclination to choose immediate rewards over future rewards, even when these immediate rewards are smaller.

So, why does this happen? Well, it's a spin-off from this bigger idea called "delay discounting." Delay discounting is basically when you think something is worth less just because you won't get it right away. If someone offered me $1,000 now or $1,400 a year from now, I may take the thousand today, even though I'd get more money later. It's like we're hardwired to be scared of the unknown and would instead settle for something certain.

The decisions you make today will impact your future.

Invest in you.

APPLICATION

What are you holding on to because of the fear of short-term pain? How will that potentially prevent you from achieving a long-term gain?

What's one action you'll take to make sure you're investing in the long-term?

Tell, text, or share this with your accountability partner or someone else.

TRANSFORMATION

> How did it feel to make that investment and what were you telling yourself during the experience?

Do you know yourself better this week than you did last week?

◯ Yes ◯ No

Did you share this week's Inspiration, Application, or Transformation with someone?

◯ Yes ◯ No

If not, do it now.

Did you complete your goal?

◯ Yes ◯ No

> **I'VE PREPARED A LIST OF RECOMMENDED BOOKS FROM PEOPLE LIKE JON ACUFF. YOU CAN CHECK OUT THAT LIST AT WWW.SKOTWALDRON.COM/BOOKS.**

---

[1] Zhang, Huaiyu & Watson-Singleton, Natalie & Pollard, Sara & Pittman, Delishia & Lamis, Dorian & Fischer, Nicole & Patterson, Bobbi & Kaslow, Nadine. (2017). "Self-Criticism and Depressive Symptoms: Mediating Role of Self-Compassion." *OMEGA - Journal of Death and Dying.* 80. 003022281772960. 10.1177/0030222817729609.

WEEK 28

CELEBRATION IS AN ESSENTIAL TOOL FOR LIFE, AS IT FORTIFIES OUR SPIRIT AND CONNECTS US TO THE VERY ESSENCE OF PURPOSE AND JOY.

INSPIRATION

We often get so engrossed in achieving our goals that we overlook the smaller victories along the way. It's not just about reaching the summit; it's also about appreciating the journey. From a neuroscience perspective, taking the time to celebrate these small wins actually rewires your brain for increased focus and motivation. Your brain tends to remember failures more easily than successes, thanks to its built-in negativity bias. However, when you consciously acknowledge and celebrate your achievements, you're sending a signal to your brain that this positive feeling is worth repeating. Remember, your brain is there to protect you, so reinforcing the idea of "safety" is critical. Celebration does just that.

Now, some people might hesitate to celebrate because they think their accomplishments are too minor to be noteworthy. This mindset misses the point. Every achievement, regardless of its size, is a building block toward greater success. Celebrating these moments can serve to increase your self-esteem and optimism, which in turn fuels your drive to take on even bigger challenges.

Next time you knock something off your to-do list or reach a mini-milestone, don't just rush past it. Pause. Give yourself some credit, and savor that winning feeling. It's not just good for the soul, it's rocket fuel for your motivation. You'll find yourself eager to conquer the next big thing. The journey is where the magic happens. Celebrate it.

APPLICATION

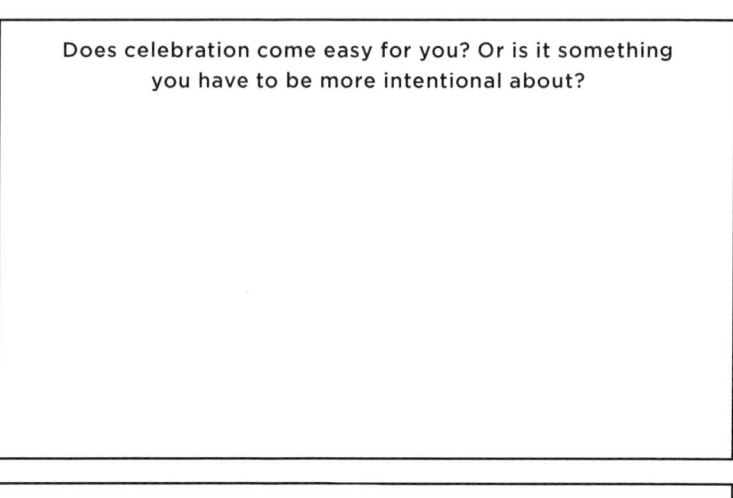

Does celebration come easy for you? Or is it something you have to be more intentional about?

What's something you can celebrate right now?

Look for moments to celebrate this week. It could be winning a big project at work or something as simple as your kids picking up their dirty socks after you asked them to.

Tell, text, or share this with your accountability partner or someone else.

TRANSFORMATION

....

> What or who do you want to celebrate from this last week?

Do you know yourself better this week than you did last week?

○ Yes ○ No

Did you share this week's Inspiration, Application, or Transformation with someone?

○ Yes ○ No

If not, do it now.

Did you complete your goal?

○ Yes ○ No

WEEK 29

RESULTS ARE NOT THE ESSENCE OF YOUR GREATNESS. THEY ARE SIMPLY THE CONFIRMATION OF IT.

INSPIRATION

Your inherent value and greatness do not stem from your achievements, accolades, or external validation but rather from your intrinsic worth, character, and personal growth.

Results and successes are merely outward manifestations, or confirmations, of the internal greatness that already exists within you. They do not define you; instead, they reflect the potential you're capable of.

Your character, your growth: these are the heroes of your narrative.

What are your achievements telling you? Those are the things you need to recognize and repeat over and over. It's the recognition of those things that will help you grow into the person you want to be.

What's really cool about all of this is those achievements are easier to spot than you might recognize. Look at your kids, look at a project you've completed, and at a minimum, look at the fact that you woke up and accomplished another day.

For me, it's my business I've been growing, molding, crashing, and rebuilding since 2010. I've learned more about myself through this epic journey than from anything else (outside of being a husband and father.)

One study delves into how self-affirmation works in the brain, using functional MRI scans for real-time observations. According to the research, when people engage in self-affirmations, such as, "I'm a really good (boss, dad, sister, volunteer, neighbor, or whatever)," the parts of their brain that deal with self-perception and self-value start lighting up. This brain activity was even linked to positive behavior changes, like increased physical activity. Self-affirmation doesn't just make you feel good; it actually changes how your brain works, potentially leading to real-world improvements in your behavior.[1]

Achievements are great, but never forget, they are really just the beautiful frame that enhances the work of art you already are.

APPLICATION

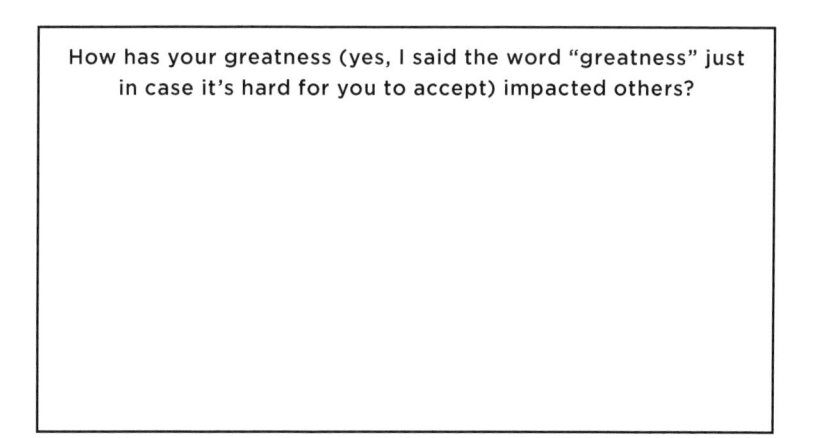

> How has your greatness (yes, I said the word "greatness" just in case it's hard for you to accept) impacted others?

> Write your "I'm a great _____" statement below, then write it on a sticky note and put it on your bathroom mirror.
> *This statement isn't about arrogance. Arrogance stems from pride and being unteachable. This statement must come from a place of humility.*

Tell, text, or share this with your accountability partner or someone else.

TRANSFORMATION

How did your greatness impact someone this past week?

Do you know yourself better this week than you did last week?

○ Yes ○ No

Did you share this week's Inspiration, Application, or Transformation with someone?

○ Yes ○ No

If not, do it now.

Did you complete your goal?

○ Yes ○ No

---

[1] Cascio CN, O'Donnell MB, Tinney FJ, Lieberman MD, Taylor SE, Strecher VJ, Falk EB. "Self-affirmation activates brain systems associated with self-related processing and reward and is reinforced by future orientation." *Soc Cogn Affect Neurosci.* 2016 Apr;11(4):621-9. doi: 10.1093/scan/nsv136. Epub 2015 Nov 5. PMID: 26541373; PMCID: PMC4814782.

WEEK 30

INSTEAD OF BEATING OURSELVES UP, WE SHOULD EXPLORE OURSELVES WITH CURIOSITY AND COMPASSION.

KRISTIN NEFF

INSPIRATION

Imagine if, instead of criticizing yourself for those slip-ups, you sat down for a drink with your thoughts and emotions. No judgment, just an open conversation.

"Hey there, Mistake. What can you teach me?"

This is the heart of vulnerability – being your own pal. It's about swapping out the hammer for a friendly handshake. It's about turning that critical eye into a curious and compassionate gaze.

Your inner world is rich, complicated, and oh-so-beautiful in its imperfection. Don't storm through it. Stroll through it.

Researchers found that being self-critical was a strong predictor for showing signs of depression, even when considering other factors. So, in plain terms, it's not just your parents' critical attitude that makes you self-critical. It's also your own tendency to worry too much about mistakes and to ruminate that leads to internalized self-criticism (ISC), which in turn can make you more likely to be depressed.[1]

At the end of the day, vulnerability is about recognizing that you're human – beautiful, flawed, and utterly unique. It's not about having all the answers; it's about asking the questions with an open heart.

Let's be curious. Let's be kind. To ourselves and each other.

APPLICATION

In which area of your life do you tend
to be most hard on yourself?

What's one action you can take
to be more curious about that?

Tell, text, or share this with your accountability partner or someone else.

TRANSFORMATION

> When you made a mistake this week, did you take the step to be both curious and compassionate?

Do you know yourself better this week than you did last week?

O Yes   O No

Did you share this week's Inspiration, Application, or Transformation with someone?

O Yes   O No

If not, do it now.

Did you complete your goal?

O Yes   O No

---

[1] Manfredi, Chiara; Caselli, Gabriele; Pescini, Federica; Rossi, Martina; Rebecchi, Daniela; Ruggiero, Giovanni Maria; and Sassaroli, Sandra. "Parental Criticism, Self-Criticism and Their Relation to Depressive Mood: An Exploratory Study Among a Non-Clinical Population" (2016) *Research in Psychotherapy*. Available at: https://www.researchinpsychotherapy.org/index.php/rpsy/article/view/178/171#toc (Accessed: 16 October 2023).

WEEK 31

YOUR EXISTENCE IS THE EVIDENCE OF YOUR VICTORIES OVER LIFE'S CHALLENGES.

INSPIRATION

You've got a streak in you that's made of steel, even if you don't always feel it. Every setback you've weathered, every obstacle you've overcome, has been more than just a test, it's been a victory, a sign that you can take whatever the mountain of life throws at you and come out stronger than before. Each of these moments has added a step to the climb of your life, and they all read, "I survived."

Think about it: every single thing you've faced, you've overcome.

That's not just luck or coincidence; it's a testament to your resilience.

Researchers found that if you're more resilient or positive, you're generally better at coping with stress, less likely to feel burned out, and more likely to stay engaged.

They also pointed out that there are two kinds of resilience: one that helps you proactively change things for the better and another that helps you hang in there when things get tough.[1]

So, look back at your past not as a series of hurdles you've had to jump but as a string of battles you've won. This isn't about romanticizing the hard times; it's about recognizing that you're stronger for having faced them.

As you move forward, don't forget this powerful fact: you are a survivor. You've faced the storm and come out the other side time and again. And you'll do it again, no matter what comes your way. After all, resilience isn't just what you do, it's who you are.

APPLICATION

What's the last hard thing you had to endure?

How did it shape you?

How will you adapt your reaction the next time you face a difficult task?

Tell, text, or share this with your accountability partner or someone else.

TRANSFORMATION

....

How did this new perspective shape your behavior this week?

Do you know yourself better this week than you did last week?

○ Yes ○ No

Did you share this week's Inspiration, Application, or Transformation with someone?

○ Yes ○ No

If not, do it now.

Did you complete your goal?

○ Yes ○ No

[1] Gabrielli, Silvia. "Cross-Sectional Study of Resilience, Positivity and Coping Strategies as Predictors of Engagement-Burnout in Undergraduate Students: Implications for Prevention and Treatment in Mental Well-Being", *Frontiers in Psychiatry,* www.frontiersin.org/articles/10.3389/fpsyt.2021.596453/full. Accessed 17 Oct. 2023.

WEEK 32

IF YOU DON'T DEFINE YOUR IDENTITY, OTHERS WILL DEFINE IT FOR YOU.

INSPIRATION

If you don't take charge and define yourself or understand your value, you risk letting the opinions and perceptions of others dictate your self-image. It's about recognizing that you are the climber of your own expedition and that your worth is not dependent on external validation. It's a nudge to invest in self-awareness, to cultivate self-belief, and to consciously understand and uphold your inherent value.

You get to decide your worth. Don't delegate that power to others.

APPLICATION

How would you describe your identity?

What do you want people to say about you when you aren't around?

Ask three people to each give you three words to describe you. Then, ask them to finish this sentence, "(Your name) is the kind of person who..."

Tell, text, or share this with your accountability partner or someone else.

TRANSFORMATION

....

> What were the words you received
> from the people you asked?

> How did they finish the sentence,
> "(Your name) is the kind of person who..."?

Do you know yourself better this week than you did last week?

○ Yes ○ No

Did you share this week's Inspiration, Application, or Transformation with someone?

○ Yes ○ No

If not, do it now.

Did you complete your goal?

○ Yes ○ No

WEEK 33

THIS WEEK, MAY YOU HAVE THE CONFIDENCE OF AN 8TH GRADER'S WISPY MUSTACHE.

JON ACUFF

INSPIRATION

Remember the subtle swagger of that school kid, the one who navigated the hallways with newfound confidence, thanks to a few wisps of hair sprouting above his upper lip? His demeanor reflected the pivotal crossroad between boyhood and manhood, and the sparse whiskers were his badge of honor. His stride was a testimony to the willingness to embrace change, to celebrate the process of maturation, and to confront the future fearlessly.

People often think that confidence is something you're born with, and if you don't have it you're out of luck. That's not the case. Confidence isn't a set trait; it's shaped by what you think and what you do. It's not even about being naturally skilled at something; it's more about believing that you can *become* skilled at it. Confidence grows from your mindset, not just your abilities.

What if you were just 1% more confident? That tiny uptick can actually inspire you to stretch your boundaries just a bit. Maybe you speak up in a meeting or tackle a project you've been dodging.

This isn't about overnight success; it's the ripple effect. These little wins, they stack up. You'll start to notice differences in various areas of your life, be it in your relationships, your job, or even just your general sense of happiness.

Confidence has this cool way of feeding itself. A small win today lays the groundwork for a bigger win tomorrow.

Imagine if you carried yourself with that level of pride in your journey of personal development. Imagine if you celebrated your milestones, regardless of how minute they seem, with the same fervor that kid celebrated his entry into manhood. It would signal your willingness to embrace change, to venture out of your comfort zone, and to truly relish your growth. Strive to emulate the spirit of that mustachioed school kid, marching forward into the future, proud of your evolution.

APPLICATION

Where is your confidence wavering?

What's one thing you can do this week
to build more confidence in that area?

Tell, text, or share this with your accountability partner or someone else.

TRANSFORMATION

Do you know yourself better this week than you did last week?

○ Yes ○ No

Are you feeling 1% more confident?

○ Yes ○ No

Did you share this week's Inspiration, Application, or Transformation with someone?

○ Yes ○ No

If not, do it now.

Did you complete your goal?

○ Yes ○ No

WEEK 34

IT'S NOT ABOUT BECOMING GREAT. IT'S ABOUT UNLOCKING THE GREATNESS ALREADY INSIDE YOU.

INSPIRATION

Step outside the confines of doubt and outdated self-perceptions, and instead, engage with the transformative power of self-belief and originality. We each have within us the capacity to create, inspire, and lead. By recognizing and honoring your inner greatness, you can fuel your capacity to make a meaningful difference.

It's time to redefine yourself, not by the limiting perceptions of others, but by the empowering realization of your own potential. It's about not just being the hiker in your own life, but taking charge as the Sherpa, steering your own course toward growth and impact. Unlock the innovator, the motivator, the leader within you, and set them free.

APPLICATION

Where do you find yourself consistently striving to be great?

Now, take that same situation and
explain where you're already great.
*Yes, there's always work to do, but stop
briefly and give yourself a little credit.*

Tell, text, or share this with your accountability partner or someone else.

TRANSFORMATION

> When did you get a chance to recognize your greatness this past week?

Do you know yourself better this week than you did last week?

○ Yes ○ No

Did you share this week's Inspiration, Application, or Transformation with someone?

○ Yes ○ No

If not, do it now.

Did you complete your goal?

○ Yes ○ No

WEEK 35

YOUR PERSONAL HEALTH IS A COMPETITIVE ADVANTAGE OR A DAILY LIABILITY.

JEREMIE KUBICEK

INSPIRATION

Can you imagine climbing Mount Everest while battling the flu? How about navigating complex tasks while grappling with anxiety or depression? Odds are, those would be far from your finest moments. It's clear that your health—physical, mental, emotional, and spiritual—plays a critical role not just in your overall well-being but also in your ability to excel.

In a systematic review, researchers dug into what affects healthcare workers' mental health and job performance, especially during something like the COVID-19 pandemic. They found nine key factors messing with both: things like feeling depressed or anxious, not getting enough support, job stress, lower productivity, not being prepared at work, money worries, fear of spreading the virus, and just plain burnout.[1] 93% of healthcare workers were experiencing stress, 86% reported experiencing anxiety, 77% reported frustration, 76% reported exhaustion and burnout, and 75% said they were overwhelmed.[2]

Not good.

Take a moment to consider health as your secret weapon. A robust state of health fuels you with the vitality, clarity, and resilience needed to dominate your professional and personal lives. On the flip side, neglecting your health doesn't just bring personal discomfort—it risks hindering your productivity, creativity, and overall performance.

Start viewing health not merely as a personal matter but as an indispensable tool for success. A strong mind in a strong body isn't just an ideal to aspire to; it's the foundation of every triumph to come.

APPLICATION

Which area of your personal health do you need to focus on?
Physical, mental, emotional, or spiritual?

What are you going to do this week
to make improvements in that area?

Tell, text, or share this with your accountability partner or someone else.

TRANSFORMATION

Do you know yourself better this week than you did last week?

○ Yes ○ No

Do you feel any better?

○ Yes ○ No

What happened?

Did you share this week's Inspiration, Application, or Transformation with someone?

○ Yes ○ No

If not, do it now.

Did you complete your goal?

○ Yes ○ No

---

[1] Nowrouzi-Kia B, Sithamparanathan G, Nadesar N, Gohar B, Ott M. "Factors associated with work performance and mental health of healthcare workers during pandemics: a systematic review and meta-analysis." *J Public Health* (Oxf). 2022 Dec 1;44(4):731-739. doi: 10.1093/pubmed/fdab173. PMID: 34056663; PMCID: PMC8194873.

[2] "The Mental Health of Healthcare Workers in COVID-19" *Mental Health America*, mhanational.org/mental-health-healthcare-workers-covid-19. Accessed 17 Oct. 2023.

WEEK 36

HOW MANY OF THE GREATEST THINGS THAT HAVE EVER HAPPENED TO ME WERE BECAUSE OF ME?

CAROLINE MYSS

INSPIRATION

Reflecting on your accomplishments can lead to a profound realization: the greatest things that have happened in your life often spring from your own actions, decisions, and attitudes. This isn't a statement of ego but a recognition of personal power and responsibility.

My wife and I gave my son a card for his birthday that said, "There's just one thing to say to someone as good-looking and as smart as you." Open card. "You're welcome." Yes, it's a little funny, but now that I think about it, it's taking pride in who we are as parents and the choices we've made to have kids and raise them the way we feel is best.

When you examine the high points in your life, you'll likely see that your choices and actions played a crucial role. It could be the decision to apply for that challenging job, the courage to ask out the person who eventually became your spouse, or the commitment to a healthier lifestyle that transformed your well-being.

While the people in your life, as well as luck, fate, or whatever you want to call it, certainly play a role, this perspective highlights the power of personal agency. It's a call to acknowledge your potential to shape your destiny. Remember, you aren't simply a passive recipient of life's unfolding narrative; you're the author, wielding a pen filled with the ink of your choices and actions.

APPLICATION

> **Reflect on some of the greatest moments in your life so far.**
> *What role did you play in those moments? Would they have happened without something you did or said? Again, this isn't intended to ignore the other people in your life who have cleared paths for you, worked for you, fought for you, mentored you, etc. You're simply acknowledging your own power in these special moments.*

Tell, text, or share this with your accountability partner or someone else.

TRANSFORMATION

> Reflect again on one of the moments you mentioned earlier. How do you feel about it now?

Do you know yourself better this week than you did last week?

○ Yes ○ No

Did you share this week's Inspiration, Application, or Transformation with someone?

○ Yes ○ No

If not, do it now.

Did you complete your goal?

○ Yes ○ No

CHECK-IN

IT'S CHECK-IN TIME!

It's that time again!

How consistent have you been? That's what you should be aiming for. If you've truly been intentional about this, the journey hasn't been easy.

That's why you should go back to Week 1 and reread that chapter. This is where a partner really comes in to help with accountability and encouragement. It's like that scene in a movie where one character is falling behind, thinking they can't make it, and the snowstorm is getting worse. Then, the other character finds the strength for both of them to keep going.

They help each other.

If you haven't already, find someone to climb this last part of the mountain with you.

You know the drill. Rate yourself here, then go back and compare your scores to your previous numbers.

Did your score improve? Don't forget that high-five!

Did you see a dip? Why? And, yes, keep it up with the high-five.

You got this.

THE TWO SIDES OF LEADERSHIP

Rate yourself from 1-10, with 1 being the lowest and 10 being the highest:

RATE HOW WELL YOU'RE PERSONALLY PERFORMING:

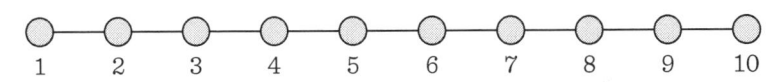

○—○—○—○—○—○—○—○—○—○
1   2   3   4   5   6   7   8   9   10

RATE HOW WELL YOU ARE LEADING OTHERS:

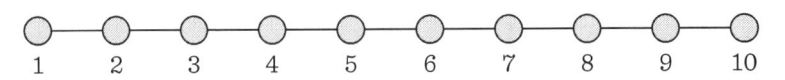

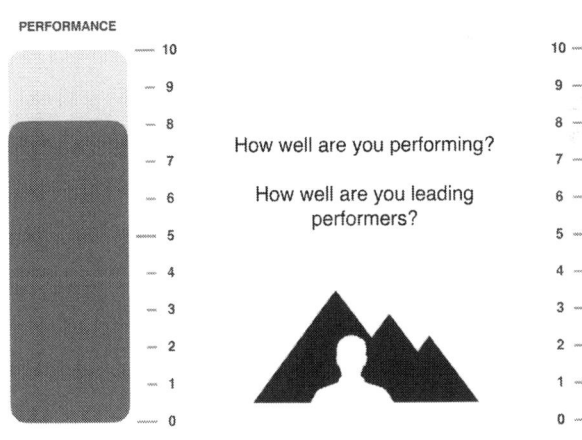

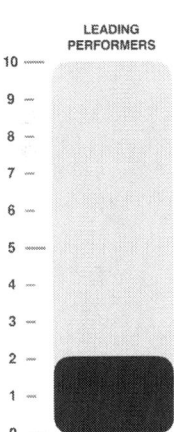

○—○—○—○—○—○—○—○—○—○
1   2   3   4   5   6   7   8   9   10

PERFORMANCE

LEADING PERFORMERS

How well are you performing?

How well are you leading performers?

GiANT

© Pub House

LOVE YOURSELF

SUPPORT AND CHALLENGE

Using the graphic below, plot yourself on the matrix. Make a dot for each circle of influence (self, family, team, organization, community). You should have at least five dots at the end of the exercise. Now, go back and compare.

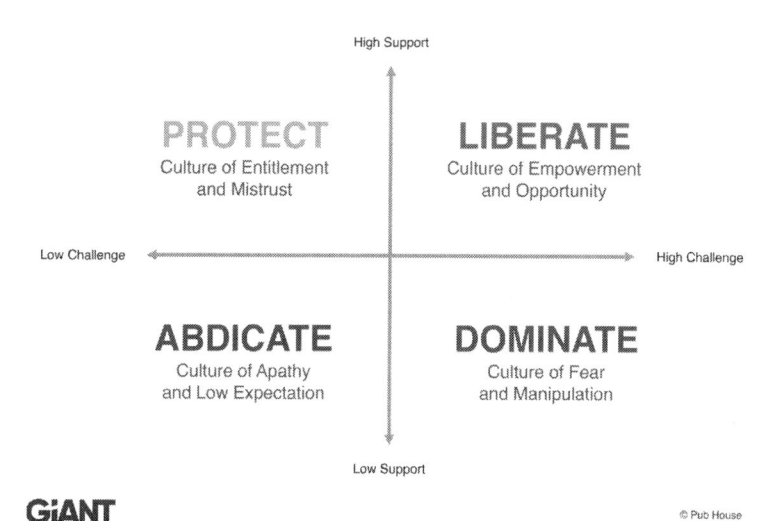

High Support

PROTECT
Culture of Entitlement
and Mistrust

LIBERATE
Culture of Empowerment
and Opportunity

Low Challenge ←——————————————→ High Challenge

ABDICATE
Culture of Apathy
and Low Expectation

DOMINATE
Culture of Fear
and Manipulation

Low Support

GiANT

© Pub House

KNOW, LOVE, LEAD

Rate yourself 1-10 on how well you know yourself, how much you love yourself, and how well you lead yourself, with 1 being the lowest score and 10 being the highest.

KNOW:

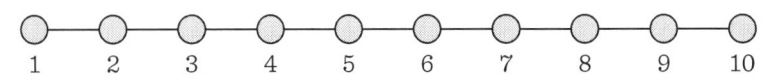

○—○—○—○—○—○—○—○—○—○
1   2   3   4   5   6   7   8   9   10

LOVE:

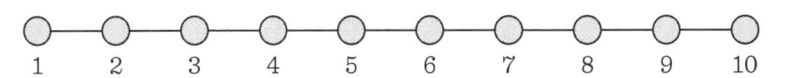

○—○—○—○—○—○—○—○—○—○
1   2   3   4   5   6   7   8   9   10

LEAD:

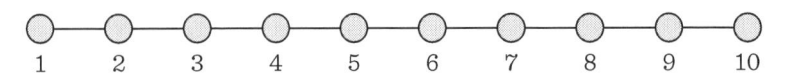

○—○—○—○—○—○—○—○—○—○
1   2   3   4   5   6   7   8   9   10

THESE ARE A FEW TOOLS OUT OF 60+ TOTAL TOOLS I USE TO COACH MY CLIENTS. GAIN ACCESS TO ALL OF THEM AT WWW.SKOTWALDRON.COM/TOOLS.

Where were you doing better or worse based on your previous evaluations?

Look at the last question of each week that asks, "Did you complete your goal?" How many did you complete?

What's going well?

Where are you struggling, and what can be done to help?

What's your biggest win of the third 12 weeks?

Who are you going to share that with, and when?

Part Three

LEAD YOURSELF

WEEK 37

STRESS: WHEN RESPONSIBILITIES OUTWEIGH CAPACITY.

DR. DAVID ALLEN

INSPIRATION

Stress. We've all been there. It's like a switch that gets flipped on when we're under pressure. And sure, in small doses, it keeps us alert and ready to take action.

But imagine keeping that switch on all the time. That's what chronic stress is like: a constant state of high alert, making your body feel like you're always on the edge. It messes with everything, from how well you sleep to how clearly you think.

According to the American Institute of Stress, approximately 77% of Americans regularly experience physical symptoms caused by stress and 73% experience psychological symptoms from stress. And how about this one: 33% of people feel they are living with extreme stress![1]

That's not good.

For leaders, self-care isn't a detour; it's the main road.

Addressing stress is not about trying to escape reality by taking your phone into the bathroom for extended periods of time. It's about making sure you're in top form to tackle stress head-on. The task at hand? To keep that stress switch in check.

APPLICATION

To alleviate stress, do you need to increase capacity or decrease responsibilities?

What are you going to do this week to make that happen?

Tell, text, or share this with your accountability partner or someone else.

TRANSFORMATION

Do you know yourself better this week than you did last week?

◯ Yes ◯ No

Did your stress reduce?

◯ Yes ◯ No

> If not, ask yourself again, do you need to increase capacity or decrease responsibilities?

Did you share this week's Inspiration, Application, or Transformation with someone?

◯ Yes ◯ No

If not, do it now.

Did you complete your goal?

◯ Yes ◯ No

---

[1]Baum, A. "Stress and Health: A Review of Psychobiological Processes," *Annual Review of Psychology* (1986).

WEEK 38

JUST AS A PARENT CAN'T BUY THE LOVE OF THEIR CHILDREN WITH GIFTS, A COMPANY CAN'T BUY THE LOYALTY OF THEIR EMPLOYEES WITH SALARIES AND BONUSES.

SIMON SINEK

INSPIRATION

To finish up this thought, Simon continues, "We will judge a boss who spends time after hours to help us as more valuable than a boss who simply gives us a bonus when we hit a target."

Think about it, what do you remember more? A boss who was there in the trenches with you, supporting you when things got tough? Or a boss who tossed a bonus your way when you nailed a project?

Sure, the bonus is great. But it's fleeting; it comes and goes. But that after-hours help, that time and effort... that's something you don't forget.

A study showed that affirmation and feedback are most effective for motivating employees to do their best work. While other themes like autonomy and inspiration surface as top motivators for employees, recognition was the most common theme that emerged from responses.[1]

This is about the type of leader you want to be and the impact you want to have on people's lives. It's not about the short-term rewards. It's about the long-term difference you make.

It's about your character. It's about being there for your team, showing them you're with them every step of the mountain-climbing adventure. Setting hooks, setting ladders, offering encouragement, and being "for them." That's the legacy that sticks. That's the stuff of great leaders. What will your legacy be?

APPLICATION

Who is someone that needs more
time and attention from you?

What are you going to do this week to make time for them?
You have the time. It's just about what you're choosing to do with it.

Tell, text, or share this with your accountability partner
or someone else.

TRANSFORMATION

> How did it feel spending more time with the individual you identified?

Do you think they found value in the time you spent together?

◯ Yes ◯ No

Do you know yourself better this week than you did last week?

◯ Yes ◯ No

Did you share this week's Inspiration, Application, or Transformation with someone?

◯ Yes ◯ No

If not, do it now.

Did you complete your goal?

◯ Yes ◯ No

---

[1] Hastwell, C. "Creating a Culture of Recognition" *Great Place To Work*, 2 Mar. 2023, www.greatplacetowork.com/resources/blog/creating-a-culture-of-recognition. Accessed 18 Oct. 2023.

WEEK 39

GRATITUDE ALWAYS EQUALS GROWTH.

INSPIRATION

Practicing gratitude - it's like emotional weightlifting. It's a decision to embrace all the feels: the good, the bad, and the ugly. And you know what? This emotional workout doesn't just make us happier; it flexes our bravery, resilience, and understanding of the world around us.

In a study done at a university counseling center, around 300 adults were divided into groups, and one group got the assignment to pen down gratitude letters for three weeks. When researchers checked back in 12 weeks after the last letter, the gratitude crew felt noticeably better mentally than those who didn't write letters.

Another gratitude exercise called "Three Good Things" had folks jot down three positive moments from their day and the reasons behind them. This simple act boosted their happiness and cut down on their blues for as long as six months after the study wrapped up.[1]

In 2020, I was hearing a lot about gratitude. Many of the people I admired had mentioned how they had some kind of gratitude practice. I wasn't feeling all that positive at that time because of COVID-19, my mother's cancer diagnosis, and some other things. I decided to write down five things I was grateful for every day, first thing in the morning, for 365 days. It took me a little over a year to complete it because I missed some days, but I did it. The cool thing about it is the app I used to journal every day reminds me of anniversaries from previous year's posts.

I'm still benefiting from that exercise. Not only am I more positive, but I tend to deflect negativity and share my positive outlook with others, hoping it will infect them with those same attitudes.

Diving headfirst into the depths of your emotions isn't for the faint of heart. It takes courage. It's an opportunity to grow, to evolve, and to march fearlessly toward a life filled with authenticity.

Not only that but expressing gratitude also strengthens your connection with others. It's the superglue in your relationships, the stuff that draws people closer together.

APPLICATION

This week, I want you to pick three people and write a thank you note to them. It doesn't have to be long. And the best part is you will write it by hand and send it in the mail! I know, it's so old school.

Write down the names of the three people and the dates when you will write each note.

Tell, text, or share this with your accountability partner or someone else.

TRANSFORMATION

> How did you feel after writing those notes?

> How do you think the recipient felt receiving them?

Do you know yourself better this week than you did last week?

◯ Yes ◯ No

Did you share this week's Inspiration, Application, or Transformation with someone?

◯ Yes ◯ No

If not, do it now.

Did you complete your goal?

◯ Yes ◯ No

---

[1] Pratt, M. "The Science of Gratitude," *Mindful,* 17 Feb. 2022, www.mindful.org/the-science-of-gratitude/. Accessed 18 Oct. 2023.

WEEK 40

DON'T JUST LOOK BACK. REACH BACK.

ALEX TREMBLE

INSPIRATION

How often are you reaching out a hand to those treading the path you once followed, offering the light of your experiences to illuminate their journey? Each stumbling block you navigated, each victory you achieved, can be a beacon for those on the journey behind you.

Leadership isn't a solo sport. It's not about being the lone wolf, miles ahead of the pack. It's about looking back, seeing who's following in your footsteps, and ensuring you're helping them along.

Every hurdle you've cleared, every summit you've reached, they're not only triumphs but signposts, telling others that they can do it too. So, take a moment to think about the legacy you're leaving. Because true leadership? That's about reaching the top and turning around to extend a hand to the next person climbing up.

APPLICATION

Who have you been mentoring lately (in life or at work) that could use a little more support from you?

What will you do to reach back out and support them this week?

Tell, text, or share this with your accountability partner or someone else.

TRANSFORMATION

> What tendencies were getting in the way of you supporting the person you identified?

Do you know yourself better this week than you did last week?

○ Yes ○ No

Did you share this week's Inspiration, Application, or Transformation with someone?

○ Yes ○ No

If not, do it now.

Did you complete your goal?

○ Yes ○ No

WEEK 41

SHAMING SOMEONE INTO ACTION CREATES ACTING. INSPIRING SOMEONE INTO ACTION CREATES CHANGE.

NEIL STRAUSS

INSPIRATION

Physically lighting a fire under someone will likely get them to move over so they don't get burned, but then they just stop again because they're out of danger. What then? You have to light another fire to get them to move. And this pattern repeats itself over and over again while at the same time, frustration becomes the norm.

Real, meaningful change? That comes from lighting a fire inside someone—it's sparked by inspiration.

Imagine a world where actions are fueled by a purpose that echoes deep within. A place where folks feel seen, appreciated, and fired up. A place where they're stirred into action not because they're scared of what might happen if they don't act but because they're excited about what could happen if they do.

Research by management consulting firm McKinsey revealed that intrinsically motivated employees (those whose internal fire is burning bright!) show 46% higher levels of job satisfaction and 32% greater levels of commitment to their jobs. At the same time, they're a lot less likely to experience job-related burnout. This all means that employees are a lot more likely to want to stick around with their employer.[1]

When actions are steered by inspiration, you're not just going through the motions—you're growing. Staying engaged becomes more than a checkbox on your to-do list; it weaves itself into the fabric of who you are.

APPLICATION

> Who have you been trying to compel into action lately by "lighting a fire under them" because they didn't seem motivated?

> How well has that been working for you and them?

> Try asking them these questions:
>
> "What activities or projects make you lose track of time?"
> - This question helps identify areas of deep interest or passion for the person, which can often be a source of intrinsic motivation.
>
> "Can you recall a time when you felt truly driven or motivated? What was it that sparked that feeling?"
> - This question can help uncover past instances of motivation, potentially revealing key factors that could motivate them again.
>
> "What values or goals are most important in your life?"
> - This question allows you to understand their core beliefs and long-term objectives, helping you determine if there's an alignment with your purpose.

Tell, text, or share this with your accountability partner or someone else.

TRANSFORMATION

> How did the conversation go when you asked those questions, and what did you learn?

Do you know yourself better this week than you did last week?

○ Yes ○ No

Did you share this week's Inspiration, Application, or Transformation with someone?

○ Yes ○ No

If not, do it now.

Did you complete your goal?

○ Yes ○ No

---

[1] "The State of Human Capital 2012—Why the human capital function still has far to go." *McKinsey.* www.mckinsey.com/capabilities/people-and-organizational-performance/our-insights/the-state-of-human-capital-2012-report. Accessed 19 Oct. 2023.

WEEK 42

1N=5P

DR. JOHN GOTTMAN

INSPIRATION

Dr. John Gottman, a big shot in the world of psychology and relationship insight, has given us the golden ratio of relationships: the "5:1 ratio", or as he calls it, "1N=5P". Let me break it down for you: For every negative interaction, you need five positive interactions to neutralize the negative one.[1]

After years spent observing couples, Gottman cracked the code of relationship stability. In a strong, enduring relationship, the scorecard of good vibes to bad ones is 5:1 when the going gets tough. For every tricky moment or harsh word, there must be five instances of love, laughter, or understanding.

My wife loves this ratio, by the way. She reminds me of it often!

Don't get me wrong, he's not saying we should shy away from the tough stuff. Sometimes, hashing things out is what needs to be done. But his point? We need a healthy dose of positivity to balance things out.

This golden ratio holds up in friendships, at the office, and around the family dinner table. Remember to invest in the power of positivity and keep that ratio in mind.

APPLICATION

You don't have to keep a tally sheet (unless you're totally into that type of thing), but I do want you to pick one person you're going to be more intentional about this week in regards to the 1N=5P.

What are some things you can do to create more positive experiences with this person?

Tell, text, or share this with your accountability partner or someone else.

TRANSFORMATION

> What tendencies were getting in the way of you having a healthy ratio? Note that this is not an invitation for you to blame the bad ratio results on someone else. Own it.

Do you know yourself better this week than you did last week?

◯ Yes ◯ No

Did you share this week's Inspiration, Application, or Transformation with someone?

◯ Yes ◯ No

If not, do it now.

Did you complete your goal?

◯ Yes ◯ No

---

[1]Benson, K. "The Magic Relationship Ratio, According to Science," *The Gottman Institute*. www.gottman.com/blog/the-magic-relationship-ratio-according-science/. Accessed 31 Oct. 2023.

WEEK 43

WE GET GOOD AT THE THINGS WE PRACTICE EVERY DAY. ARE YOU PRACTICING SELF-AWARENESS AND SELF-CARE? OR, ARE YOU PRACTICING ACCIDENTAL LIVING, SURVIVING, AND REACTING TO EVERYTHING AND EVERYONE AROUND YOU?

INSPIRATION

Have you ever considered what actions or communication habits you're practicing each day? Are you setting aside golden moments to truly check in with yourself, caring for your emotions like they are something that deserves that kind of attention? Or are you just responding to life's avalanches, feeling dumped on by your circumstances?

The proactive system in your brain is your mental organizer, relying on fluid intelligence to connect the dots of various moving parts and come up with a streamlined game plan. Meanwhile, the reactive system is your improvisational genius. It's your mental agility that enables you to navigate that surprise avalanche.

The things you do daily, the routines you roll out, they shape who you are and who you're becoming. Your habits, they're like a playlist on repeat, and they can either be your greatest hits or just some tired old tracks that keep you stuck in the same old groove.

Take control of the tunes you're playing. Living in a reactive state all the time is not what you're built for. Consciously choose to do things that don't just keep you alive, but help you thrive. You aren't just living your life, you're creating it. And every single day is another chance to shape your future self. Crank up the volume on the good stuff.

APPLICATION

Where have you been more reactionary lately?

What are you going to do to take back more control and live more intentionally this week? Is it about setting up boundaries with others? Is it about more positive self-talk?

Tell, text, or share this with your accountability partner or someone else.

TRANSFORMATION

> What tendencies were getting in the way of you living more proactively, rather than reacting to people and situations around you?

Do you know yourself better this week than you did last week?

◯ Yes ◯ No

Did you share this week's Inspiration, Application, or Transformation with someone?

◯ Yes ◯ No

If not, do it now.

Did you complete your goal?

◯ Yes ◯ No

WEEK 44

EVERY ACTION WE TAKE IS LIKE A VOTE FOR THE TYPE OF PERSON WE WANT TO BECOME.

JAMES CLEAR

INSPIRATION

Imagine your life as a ballot box, with each action serving as a vote for the person you want to become. Some votes might pull you toward your purpose, while others might set you off course. But you're in control. Every vote is yours to cast.

What we're talking about here isn't just making decisions at random. It's about making intentional choices that align with the vision of your best self, your 'why.' It's about acknowledging that your actions don't just decide your path; they define who you are and the mark you leave on this world.

Every day, you're casting votes. Make sure they're for the candidate you believe in most – the best version of you. It's not just about making decisions; it's about shaping your identity and molding the impact you'll have on others.

I've had times in my life where I hoped all of the ballots would be thrown out, but in the election of life, that doesn't happen. Every ballot is counted, every time.

A study by Henk Aarts, Peter Gollwitzer, and Ran Hassin that landed in the Journal of Personality and Social Psychology back in 2004 shows that just by watching someone work on a goal, you're more likely to take on that same goal yourself. For instance, they had people read a story about someone working to make money. As a result, those readers were suddenly more tuned in to money-making opportunities and even put in the effort to chase them, compared to those who read a different kind of story.[1]

Our actions matter.

APPLICATION

Name the last three actions you took that had a positive or negative impact on someone.

Name three actions you'll take this week that are a vote for the person you want to become.

Tell, text, or share this with your accountability partner or someone else.

TRANSFORMATION

> What tendencies were getting in the way of taking the action you wanted to take?

Do you know yourself better this week than you did last week?

◯ Yes ◯ No

Did you share this week's Inspiration, Application, or Transformation with someone?

◯ Yes ◯ No

If not, do it now.

Did you complete your goal?

◯ Yes ◯ No

> **HAVE YOU CHECKED OUT MY LIST OF RECOMMENDED BOOKS YET? YES, JAMES CLEAR'S BOOK IS ON THAT LIST! YOU CAN CHECK IT OUT AT WWW.SKOTWALDRON.COM/BOOKS.**

[1] Aarts, H., Gollwitzer, P. M., & Hassin, R. R. (2004). "Goal Contagion: Perceiving Is for Pursuing." *Journal of Personality and Social Psychology,* 87(1), 23–37. https://doi.org/10.1037/0022-3514.87.1.23

WEEK 45

THE AMOUNT OF EFFORT YOU PUT INTO SOMEONE IS DIRECTLY TIED TO YOUR BELIEF IN THEM.

JOHN C. MAXWELL

INSPIRATION

You can't fake your belief in someone. When you invest time, energy, and resources into others, you are essentially affirming your faith in their capabilities and their capacity to grow and lead. It's like saying, "Hey, I see you, I believe in you, and I know you're capable of great things."

This isn't about handing out charity; it's about recognizing their inherent value and acknowledging the transformative power they hold.

Your thoughts aren't just random firing neurons; they're steeped in deep-seated beliefs about how relationships should work. That mental blueprint guides how you act and react to others. Depending on what you believe, you might deal with your emotions in a way that pulls you closer or pushes you further away from someone.

I am asking you to be open to possibilities, yet still grounded in the realities of what you need and know about the situation.

If you can't believe in them, then they deserve someone who does.

Leaders become great not because of their power but because of their ability to empower others.

APPLICATION

> Are you lacking faith in someone right now? If so, who?

> How have your actions reaffirmed your lack of faith in them?

> What needs to happen for you to either build more faith in them or put more effort into the relationship?

> When will you take some time to work on this?

Tell, text, or share this with your accountability partner or someone else.

TRANSFORMATION

> What tendencies were getting in the way of taking the action you wanted to take?

Do you know yourself better this week than you did last week?

○ Yes   ○ No

Did you share this week's Inspiration, Application, or Transformation with someone?

○ Yes   ○ No

If not, do it now.

Did you complete your goal?

○ Yes   ○ No

WEEK 46

I HAVE THE PERFECT AMOUNT OF TIME FOR THE THINGS THAT MATTER MOST.

INSPIRATION

This isn't about squeezing an extra hour out of thin air or hunting down a hidden stash of minutes. It's about owning up to a truth: you're the one in charge. Your focus, your energy, your treasured seconds, they're at your command, waiting for orders.

Stop telling yourself and everyone else, "I don't have time." You do have time.

You are the source of your time.

The to-do list? That's your domain. You have the power to align your day-to-day with your goals and visions. Prioritizing is your secret weapon, not a burdensome task. It's your ticket to building your life's journey, brick by precious brick.

What you really may be saying is:
- I haven't made time.
- I don't know how to make time.
- I don't want to make time.
- I don't have time to do that and keep all my other commitments.
- I'm not willing to sacrifice any of my current priorities in order to make room for this one.

Saying, "I don't have time," is you giving up control.

Take back control.

The way you spend your time is a reflection of your priorities. If something is important to you, you will find a way to fit it into your schedule.

You do have time.

Be purposeful, driven, and intentional with your time. Not a victim of it.

APPLICATION

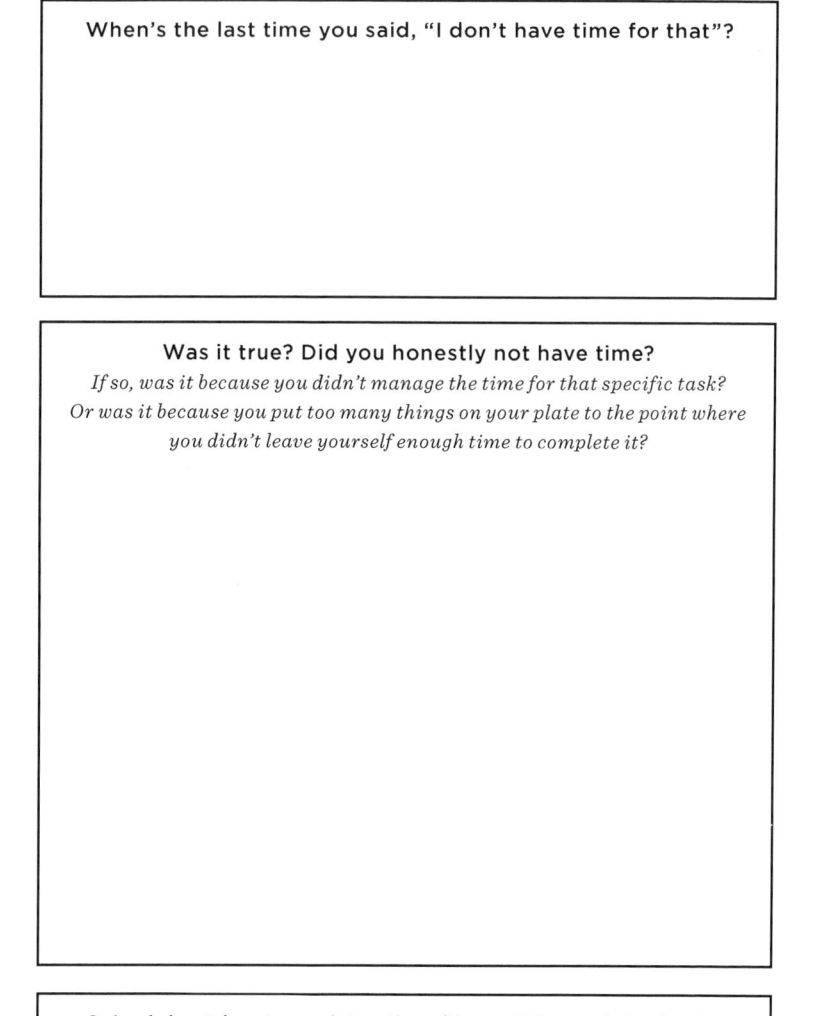

When's the last time you said, "I don't have time for that"?

Was it true? Did you honestly not have time?
If so, was it because you didn't manage the time for that specific task? Or was it because you put too many things on your plate to the point where you didn't leave yourself enough time to complete it?

Schedule at least one intentional hour this week to do the thing you need to do. That could be recharging, running an errand you've been putting off, or getting something done where you completely shut off all distractions.

> When will you take some time to work on this?

Tell, text, or share this with your accountability partner or someone else.

TRANSFORMATION

> What tendencies or situations were getting in the way of you honoring that hour?

Do you know yourself better this week than you did last week?

○ Yes ○ No

Did you share this week's Inspiration, Application, or Transformation with someone?

○ Yes ○ No

If not, do it now.

Did you complete your goal?

○ Yes ○ No

WEEK 47

ANGER WITHOUT ACTION LEADS TO BITTERNESS.

TONY ROBBINS

INSPIRATION

Anger isn't the villain it's often made out to be. Like every other feeling in our emotional repertoire, it's got a job to do. When that fiery sensation starts to bubble up, it's like a neon sign flashing, "Hey, something's not right here!"

Maybe somebody's stomped all over your boundaries, maybe your values have taken a hit, or perhaps your inner justice radar is pinging. Whatever it is, anger is there to tell you that it's time to pay attention.

It's not about the anger itself; it's about what we do with it.

In Daniel Goleman's book, *Emotional Intelligence* he says that our emotions are like pre-programmed action plans, baked into us by evolution to help us navigate life. When you get mad, your blood rushes to your hands, priming you to throw a punch or grab something to defend yourself. Your heart races and adrenaline floods your system, supercharging you for some kind of bold move. So in a way, anger is wired into our brain as a built-in security system.[1]

But if we let anger simmer, it morphs into bitterness, and that never helped anyone. It can block our path to growth and damage our leadership potential.

Channeling that anger into action is where the magic happens. You can flip the script and turn this so-called 'negative' emotion into a launching pad for change. It's about harnessing that raw energy and putting it to work for good. It's not about dodging the tough emotions; it's about learning how to ride the wave and come out stronger on the other side.

Anger shows you care.

Anger can push you to right a wrong.

Anger is part of our moral framework.

APPLICATION

> What are you angry or dissatisfied with right now?

> What's one thing you can do this week to turn that emotion into action?

> When will you execute this?

Tell, text, or share this with your accountability partner or someone else.

TRANSFORMATION

> How did you feel taking action rather than letting the emotion fester?

Do you know yourself better this week than you did last week?

◯ Yes   ◯ No

Did you share this week's Inspiration, Application, or Transformation with someone?

◯ Yes   ◯ No

If not, do it now.

Did you complete your goal?

◯ Yes   ◯ No

---

[1] Daniel Goleman – Emotional Intelligence, Social Intelligence, Ecological Intelligence" www.danielgoleman.info. Accessed 31 Oct. 2023.

WEEK 48

INSTEAD OF ASKING, "ARE YOU SURE?" YOU CAN ASK, "HOW SURE ARE YOU?"

INSPIRATION

When you throw out the question, "Are you sure?" it's like lobbing a hot potato at someone. It's a yes-or-no deal and often seems like you're questioning their conviction, putting them on the back foot.

What about asking, "How sure are you?" instead? It's like pulling up a chair and inviting them to share their story. This way, they get to walk you through their thought process, laying out the breadcrumbs that led them to their conclusion. It's more about leaning in with genuine curiosity than throwing doubt on their certainty.

Swap the interrogation for a nice conversation. Not only will it lead to better understanding, but it'll also make your conversations richer.

APPLICATION

> Pay attention this week when you question someone's thought, belief, or idea.
>
> Instead of asking, "Are you sure?" or moving straight to critique, ask, "How sure are you? Do you mind walking me through your thought process?"

Tell, text, or share this with your accountability partner or someone else.

TRANSFORMATION

> How did it go when you questioned someone's thought, belief, or idea in a new way?

Do you know yourself better this week than you did last week?

○ Yes ○ No

Did you share this week's Inspiration, Application, or Transformation with someone?

○ Yes ○ No

If not, do it now.

Did you complete your goal?

○ Yes ○ No

WEEK 49

WE CONFUSE MOTION FOR PROGRESS AND SPEED FOR DIRECTION.

DAVE ANDERSON

INSPIRATION

We live in a world where being busy is seen as a trophy. The busier you are, the more important you must be, right? Wrong. That's like saying the more noise you make, the better the music.

There's nothing wrong with a full schedule or being ambitious. But when you're racing around chasing the illusion of productivity, you're paying a hefty price. We're talking stress, burnout, and doing a disservice to your work and relationships.

U.S.A. Today published a multi-year poll in 2008 to determine how people perceived time and their own busyness. It found that in each consecutive year since 1987, people reported that they are busier than the year before, with 69% responding that they were either "busy" or "very busy" and only 8% responding that they were "not very busy." Not surprisingly, women reported being busier than men, and those between the ages of 30 and 60 were the busiest. When the respondents were asked what they were sacrificing to their busyness, 56% cited sleep, 52% recreation, 51% hobbies, 44% friends, and 30% family. In 1987, 50% said they ate at least one family meal every day; by 2008, that figure had declined to 20%.

In their study published in the Journal of Consumer Research, Paharia and her team argue that "being busy" has morphed into a status symbol. The paper, titled "Conspicuous Consumption of Time: When Busyness and Lack of Leisure Time Become a Status Symbol," points out that claiming to have a jam-packed schedule, whether it's true or not, elevates how important people think you are. Particularly in American culture, this "busy bragging" or "humble bragging" about having no free time is on the rise, according to the researchers.[1]

Our definition of "busy" may be destroying our relationships, businesses, and way of life.

Busy isn't the same as effective. True productivity is about doing things that matter. It's about lining up your efforts with your values and goals, not just ticking off tasks on a to-do list (although that can sometimes be gratifying).

So, try to shift from simply being busy to being purposefully active. Focus on actions that truly contribute to your growth.

APPLICATION

Look at your calendar. Are the things on there contributing to your overall personal and/or professional growth?

○ Yes   ○ No

Do you have a good mix of things you WANT to do and things you HAVE to do?

○ Yes   ○ No

What could you change to focus more
on what you want to be doing?

Tell, text, or share this with your accountability partner or someone else.

TRANSFORMATION

Did you fill your calendar or empty time with meaningful things this week?

○ Yes   ○ No

Do you know yourself better this week than you did last week?

○ Yes   ○ No

Did you share this week's Inspiration, Application, or Transformation with someone?

○ Yes   ○ No

If not, do it now.

Did you complete your goal?

○ Yes   ○ No

IF YOU'D LIKE TO HEAR MORE BRILLIANCE FROM DAVE, VISIT WWW.SKOTWALDRON.COM/DAVE.

[1] Bellezza, Silvia; Paharia, Neeru; and Keinan, Anat. "Conspicuous Consumption of Time: When Busyness and Lack of Leisure Time Become a Status Symbol," *Journal of Consumer Research,* 4 May 2017, www0.gsb.columbia.edu/mygsb/faculty/research/pubfiles/19293/Conspicuous%20Consumption%20of%20Time.pdf. Accessed 21 Oct. 2023.

WEEK 50

MASSIVE VS. PASSIVE ACTION

BROOKE CASTILLO

INSPIRATION

We've got two kinds of action we deal with: passive action and massive action, each useful for different parts of the journey.

Passive action is when you're busy absorbing information, laying out plans, and doing all that strategic thinking. It's necessary stuff. No one's going to tackle a mountain without first understanding the route. That's your map-checking, gear-prepping stage.

I love taking passive action. I love researching and exploring alternative ways of doing things. I love seeing how we can make things more innovative or unique. I love creating options and seeing all of the ideas I've accumulated. I even love the process of mapping it out and discussing the whole idea.

Massive action is that all-in, give-it-everything-you've-got stage. It's taking the big strides, making the bold decisions, and sticking with them even when the slope is steep and the wind is against you. It's when you take everything from the passive action stage and make it a reality. Massive action is the thing that moves the needle.

I want to love this stage as well. Massive action is where the trail actually gets blazed. The truth is, because of my own fear, insecurities, and discomfort at times, I hesitate. I continue researching and exploring, falsely labeling my behavior as massive action when, in reality, I'm still safely in the passive action stage.

You need both to complete the journey. Passive action is all about preparation, while massive action is about execution. Remember, a great journey isn't just about reading the map. It's about moving forward, one determined step at a time.

APPLICATION

> Where are you taking passive action right now?

> What massive action do you need to take?

> When will you take the massive action just mentioned?

Tell, text, or share this with your accountability partner or someone else.

TRANSFORMATION

....

> What was the result of the massive action?
> How did it compare to passive action?

Do you know yourself better this week than you did last week?

◉ Yes ◯ No

Did you share this week's Inspiration, Application, or Transformation with someone?

◉ Yes ◯ No

If not, do it now.

Did you complete your goal?

◉ Yes ◯ No

WEEK 51

WHEN WE PRIORITIZE, WE GIVE LIFE TO OUR DREAMS, SUBSTANCE TO OUR VISIONS, AND POWER TO OUR ACTIONS.

LAO TZU

INSPIRATION

It's like having a GPS for your dreams, taking them from the realm of "I wish" to "let's do this." Prioritizing isn't just about ordering your tasks—it's about giving your dreams direction, making them reachable targets instead of cloudy concepts.

Oftentimes, we fall under the spell of distraction or allow ourselves to be interrupted constantly by a ding from our cell phones or to be reachable at all times. If this is the case for you, you'll never reach the summit within your allowed time.

"Mount Everest protrudes into the stratosphere, and most of the year, the summit is buffeted by winds of over 100 miles per hour that will kill a climber in minutes or even hurtle them into the void," John All, a geographer at Western Kentucky University, told *Popular Mechanics*. "It is only during the onset or cession of the Asian Monsoon that these winds die down and allow climbers short seven- to 10-day windows to climb the mountain."[1]

When you only have that amount of time to reach the summit, every distraction and interruption is a problem.

What if we went from simply "scheduling tasks" to thinking in terms of "performance episodes," discrete time blocks dedicated to specific tasks? This concept, developed by Georgia Tech organizational psychologist Howard Weiss, emphasizes the cost of interruptions—research shows it takes about 25 minutes to refocus after a disruption.[2]

"Deep work" and "flow" states of complete absorption in a task that allow for optimal performance and skill development are concepts from positive psychologist Mihaly Csikszentmihalyi and computer scientist Cal Newport. These ideas highlight the necessity of sustained, uninterrupted focus for personal and professional growth.

Prioritizing does more than keep you organized. It means putting your goals front and center. Prioritizing is your ticket to action, to taking those dreams and making them come alive with every task you tick off.

Don't get stuck on the mountain in a storm. Prioritize your health, your dreams, and your goals. You'll be better off for it, as will everyone you live and work with.

APPLICATION

Write down what you think your top five priorities in life SHOULD be according to what you believe society expects of you.

Write down what you WANT your top five priorities to be.

> Now, write down what they actually ARE.

Compare those three lists.
What if you had six months, one year, or five years to live?
Are your priorities in line?

> What's one thing you will prioritize this week that isn't currently getting your attention?

> When are you going to take action?

Tell, text, or share this with your accountability partner or someone else.

TRANSFORMATION

....

> Was it easy to shift your focus? Why or why not?

> What was the tendency fighting against you prioritizing that thing?

Do you know yourself better this week than you did last week?

◯ Yes ◯ No

Did you share this week's Inspiration, Application, or Transformation with someone?

◯ Yes ◯ No

If not, do it now.

Did you complete your goal?

◯ Yes ◯ No

---

[1] Goodier, R. "Why Does Everyone Climb Everest in May?" 21 May 2012, www.popularmechanics.com/adventure/outdoors/a7725/why-does-everyone-climb-everest-in-may-9035510/. Accessed 1 Nov. 2023.

[2] Beal DJ, Weiss HM, Barros E, MacDermid SM. "An episodic process model of affective influences on performance." *J Appl Psychol*. 2005 Nov;90(6):1054-68. doi: 10.1037/0021-9010.90.6.1054. PMID: 16316265.

WEEK 52

LEADERSHIP ISN'T ONE BIG THING. IT'S THOUSANDS OF LITTLE THINGS EVERY DAY.

DAVE RAMSEY

INSPIRATION

Leadership is a mixture of tiny actions, daily decisions, and everyday behaviors. It's in the kindness you sprinkle around, the responsibility you stand by, the trust you cement, and the dreams you broadcast.

Each of these moments, no matter how small, is like a thread. Now, a single thread might not seem like much. But bundle them together, weave them into a tapestry, and you've got something pretty impressive. This is the fabric of real leadership.

As of August 2023, Gallup reported that only 23% of people trust their organization's leadership.

When you've got leaders and bosses who are trustworthy and really know how to inspire the team, it changes things. People click with the culture, find their work more meaningful, and generally do better on the performance front. If your team members really trust the higher-ups, they're four times as likely to be all-in at work and 58% less likely to be scrolling through job listings.[1]

A leader isn't just sitting behind a desk barking orders; they're more like a Sherpa setting you up to reach the summit. They're the ones who talk straight, have your back, and create the sort of environment where people can't help but collaborate and think outside the box.

Many employees feel like their managers are dropping the ball on this. The solution? Managerial training that focuses on turning bosses into coaches. That's how you get a leadership style that takes everyone to the next level.

Your journey through leading yourself and others will not be successfully pulled off by a grand gesture. It will take place over time and through being consistent, being authentic, being vulnerable, and being you.

APPLICATION

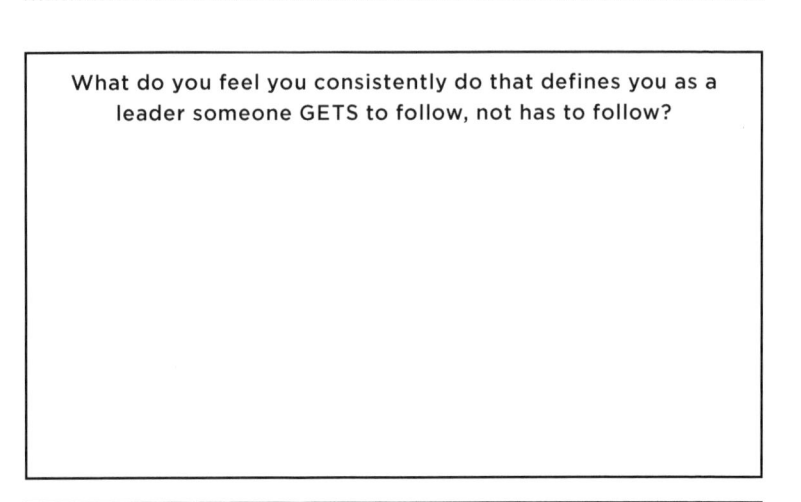

What do you feel you consistently do that defines you as a leader someone GETS to follow, not has to follow?

What is one little thing you can do every day this week to build more consistency in your leadership journey?

When are you going to take action?

Tell, text, or share this with your accountability partner or someone else.

TRANSFORMATION

> Was it easy to remain consistent? Why or why not?

Do you know yourself better this week than you did last week?

○ Yes ○ No

Did you share this week's Inspiration, Application, or Transformation with someone?

○ Yes ○ No

If not, do it now.

Did you complete your goal?

○ Yes ○ No

---

[1] Gallup. "Leadership & Management" Gallup, 3 Nov. 2022, www.gallup.com/404252/indicator-leadership-management.aspx. Accessed 21 Oct. 2023.

CHECK-IN

IT'S CHECK-IN TIME!

Here it is. The final check-in.

I don't know if it's taken you exactly 52 weeks to get here or if you've been on this expedition for years. It doesn't matter. What matters is the fact that you've arrived.

Rate yourself here, then go back and compare this to your previous check-in numbers. For example, think about the trend of the numbers. Did they start out strong at first, take a dip, then climb back up? I see this often with people I coach. I call it the "awareness dip." Sometimes, there's a lack of self-awareness early on, then the more aware people become, the more real the numbers get. That's why there's oftentimes a dip. Then, as people improve over time, they see those numbers climb again higher than they were before.

Did your numbers climb throughout the year? Was there a decline? What about the Support/Challenge Matrix? Did you stay consistently within a certain quadrant or did you move around?

Numbers are just numbers. I want you to think about what they are telling you. I've asked you a few more questions below that will help you tell more of that story.

I'm proud of you.

You should also be proud of you, too.

THE TWO SIDES OF LEADERSHIP

Rate yourself from 1-10, with 1 being the lowest and 10 being the highest:

RATE HOW WELL YOU'RE PERSONALLY PERFORMING:

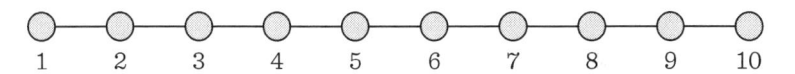

1　2　3　4　5　6　7　8　9　10

RATE HOW WELL YOU ARE LEADING OTHER PERFORMERS:

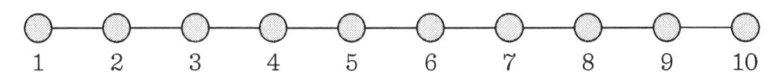

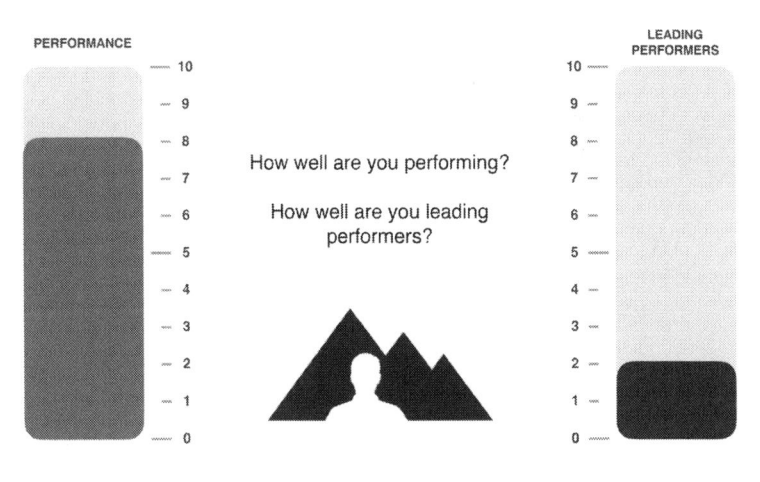

1　2　3　4　5　6　7　8　9　10

PERFORMANCE

How well are you performing?

How well are you leading performers?

LEADING PERFORMERS

GiANT

© Pub House

LEAD YOURSELF

SUPPORT AND CHALLENGE

This will be the last time. Using the graphic below, plot yourself on the matrix. Make a dot for each circle of influence (self, family, team, organization, community). You should have at least five dots at the end of the exercise.

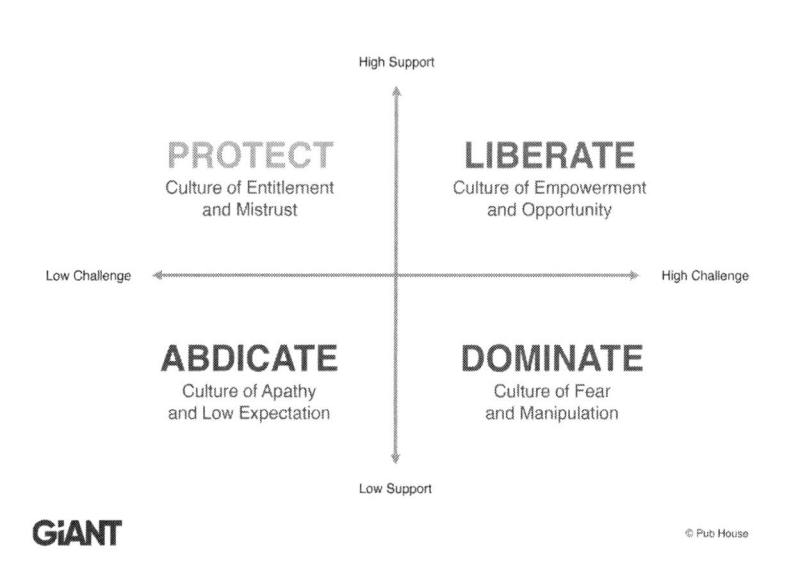

	High Support	
PROTECT		**LIBERATE**
Culture of Entitlement and Mistrust		Culture of Empowerment and Opportunity
Low Challenge ←		→ High Challenge
ABDICATE		**DOMINATE**
Culture of Apathy and Low Expectation		Culture of Fear and Manipulation
	Low Support	

KNOW, LOVE, LEAD

Rate yourself 1-10 on how well you know yourself, how much you love yourself, and how well you lead yourself, with 1 being the lowest score and 10 being the highest.

KNOW:

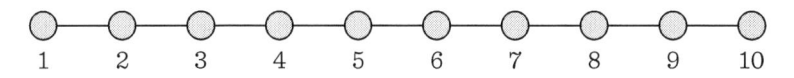

1 — 2 — 3 — 4 — 5 — 6 — 7 — 8 — 9 — 10

LOVE:

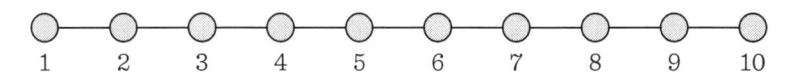

1 — 2 — 3 — 4 — 5 — 6 — 7 — 8 — 9 — 10

LEAD:

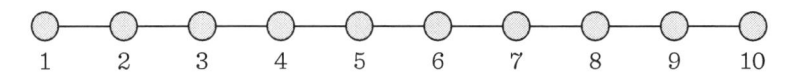

1 — 2 — 3 — 4 — 5 — 6 — 7 — 8 — 9 — 10

Where were you doing better or worse based on your previous evaluations?

Look at the last question of each week that asks, "Did you complete your goal?" How many did you complete?

What's went well?

Where did you struggle?

What's your biggest win of the entire journey?

Who are you going to share that with, and when?

THE FINAL CHAPTER

THE FINAL CHAPTER

Or is it? As my friend Steve Cockram, one of the founders of GiANT, says, "You never graduate from the school of self-awareness." It's a lifelong journey that will continue to be shaped by you and the people in your life.

As you conclude this year-long voyage of self-discovery, introspection, and leadership, let's pause for a moment of reflection. It's been a journey like no other, hasn't it? Over time, you've dissected ideas, explored perspectives, and unraveled the layers of your being. You've pondered questions that have dug deep into your thoughts, beliefs, and aspirations. You've engaged in activities that have pushed your boundaries, challenging you to evolve into a more intentional, self-aware individual.

Throughout these pages, you've embarked on a quest to know yourself better, to develop a deeper appreciation for your unique strengths, and to identify areas where growth was necessary. It's a path that requires courage, honesty, and vulnerability. The fact that you're here, at the end of this journey, is a testament to your resilience and commitment to personal growth.

More importantly, you've learned the power of loving yourself more and its vital role in your overall well-being and success. Self-love is more than a feel-good mantra. It's the foundation on which we build a fulfilled life. It's about respecting your journey, acknowledging your growth, and recognizing that every step you've taken, however small, is a move toward becoming the best version of yourself.

And then there's the intentional leadership. You've embraced the concept that leading isn't about dominating or ruling from the top. Instead, it's about nurturing, inspiring, and influencing, whether you are doing it for others or in your own life. You've discovered that leadership is a daily practice of small but impactful actions and decisions.

As we wrap up this expedition, remember that the end of this book is not the end of your journey. It's a checkpoint, a time to regroup, reflect, and celebrate your progress. Your journey of knowing yourself, loving who you are, and leading yourself more intentionally will continue. The insights you've gleaned and the growth you've achieved have equipped you to navigate the path ahead with more clarity, confidence, and purpose.

Remember, every day is a new opportunity to learn, to love, and to lead. Take the lessons you've learned here, apply them daily, and continue cultivating a life filled with growth, joy, and purpose. Here's to the journey ahead—the journey to a more authentic, fulfilled, and empowered you.

NEXT STEPS

Reaching the end of the book doesn't mean the end of your adventure; in fact, it's just another base camp on your lifelong climb. Take a moment to savor your progress, reflect on the lessons learned, and appreciate the person you've become.

Here are some ideas for the next steps you could take:

Seek advanced resources: If a specific topic or area really piqued your interest, look for more specialized books, courses, or seminars to deepen your understanding. I have a few things you can check out at the end of this book.

Bring your knowledge to work: Start a group at work where each week, you read a chapter of this book together and help to hold each other accountable to your weekly goals.

Reflect and reassess: Take a moment to reflect on the most impactful lessons you've learned. Reassess your personal and professional goals based on your newfound knowledge.

Journal your journey: Document your experiences, challenges overcome, and areas that still need work. This journal can serve as your personal roadmap for the future.

Set new goals: Now that you've reached this milestone, it's time to set your sights on new peaks to climb. Break these down into achievable steps to keep the momentum going.

Share your insights: Consider discussing your experiences and lessons learned with friends, family, or colleagues. Your journey might inspire them to undertake their own.

Mentor or coach others: Use your new skills and insights to help others. Whether in your professional network or your personal life, act as a guide for those beginning their own climb.

Revisit and refresh: After some time has passed, re-read the book or go through your journal. You'll likely find new insights that you missed the first time around.

Apply in real time: Don't let your new knowledge gather dust. Apply it to your current projects or challenges and observe the results.

Join a community: Whether online or in real life, join groups or forums where like-minded individuals gather. Share, learn, and grow together.

Celebrate your wins: Don't forget to celebrate your progress. Rewarding yourself makes the journey worthwhile and motivates you for future challenges.

Feedback loop: Get feedback from people who've been impacted by your growth—be it personal or professional. Use their insights for continued self-improvement.

Plan your next read: The end of one book should be the beginning of another. Keep the learning cycle going by choosing your next read. Need some suggestions? Email me at skot@skotwaldron.com

Act now: Don't lose the momentum. Take immediate action, no matter how small, to apply what you've learned and move toward your new goals.

You're in a powerful position to lift others up and help them along their own journeys. Maybe that means mentoring, volunteering, or even just being a more empathetic friend or family member. Your new heights of self-love don't just elevate you; they lift up everyone around you. So, as you plan your next climb, remember: the view is great, but it's even better when enjoyed with others.

CAN YOU HELP ME OUT WITH A REVIEW?

As you close this book, I hope you're walking away with actionable insights and a renewed sense of purpose. If you've found value in these pages, learned something new, or feel better equipped to tackle your personal and professional challenges, I'd love to hear from you.

Reviews are the lifeblood of any book's success, providing valuable feedback for authors. More importantly, your thoughts can help future readers to decide if this book is the right fit for their own journey.

Please take a few minutes to leave a review on Amazon. Share what you found most impactful and how you plan to implement the principles you've learned. Every review matters, and I genuinely appreciate your time and thoughts.

Thank you!

PLEASE REVIEW THE BOOK HERE:

THANKS FOR LEAVING A REVIEW!
Visit skotwaldron.com/review

ABOUT THE AUTHOR

That's "Skot" with a "K" and one "T." And no, he's not Scandinavian.

As a way to differentiate himself in the 6th grade from two other "Scott Ws," he started spelling his name "Skot," and he never had to put his last name on his papers again.

This creative, out-of-the-box thinking is what has helped Skot to develop and conduct unique strategic communication programs for companies like JP Morgan Chase, Sesame Workshop, Chiquita, The Coca-Cola Company, Cisco, Mount Sinai Hospital, and the CDC.

When he's not coaching leaders and teams on effective communication strategies or recording one of his Unlocked with Skot Waldron podcast episodes, you'll find Skot speaking on stages nationwide. He has presented to thousands of people at conferences, colleges, and companies, including SXSW, The University of North Georgia, Texas A&M, The Home Depot, Pandora Radio, and Elavon, to name just a few.

Skot lives with his wife (who's super awesome, beautiful, and smart) and two kids, Tallulah and Malan (who are also super awesome, beautiful, and smart), outside of Atlanta, Georgia.

ACKNOWLEDGMENTS

The end of one journey and the beginning of another. This book, my Everest of sorts, couldn't have been conquered without an amazing team, each playing a vital role in this expedition.

To my family, the unwavering base camp in my life — thank you. You're always there supporting and challenging me every step of the way.

A tip of the hat to Mark Goulston, a true mentor who has given his time and wisdom so freely to me this year and inspired me to take action.

To my designer, Liz Butler, for visually capturing the essence of my words and blessing me with your brilliance all of these years.

To Gabriella Williams, my editor and navigator, thank you for meticulously charting this course with me, ensuring no detail was overlooked.

A big shout-out to my colleagues and friends, the cheerleaders on the sidelines. Your cheers and honesty were the winds in my sails.

A round of applause for my launch team and beta readers (listed on the next page). Your insights were the compass that kept this journey on track.

And finally, to you, the reader, for joining me on this adventure. Your quest for growth is the reason these words now live and breathe. Here's to our shared journey toward unlocking the greatness that lies within each of us.

ADDITIONAL THANKS TO:

Bryce Ashcraft, Chandler Baker, Shon Barnwell, Alexandre Bassora, Whitney Black, David Blake, Karla Brandau, Travis Brown, Phil Buckley, Michelle Campbell, Chris Cardona, David Carl, Jennifer Chapman, Hope Chernak, Wendi Grier Chitwood, Bobby Cornwell, Pam Cusick, Shraddah Dubey, Martina Duemler, S. Chris Edmonds, Chantalle Edmunds, Mike Erwin, Andrew Freedman, Lisa Gable, Molly Gaines-McCollom, Maria Gordon, Christy Haggard, Tom Henninger, Jeanne Hey, Michelle Holton, Lorretta Jackson-Brown, Sarah Jayne, Bruce Jensen, Whitney Johnson, Kim Johnson, Jim Johnson, Kristin Kaufman, Satheesh Kumar, Suzi Lantz, Ryan Matlock, O'Brien McMahon, Amanda Merrell, Wesley Michael, Tonille Miller, Reade Milner, Barry Moltz, Alma Morales, Shane Mullen, Greg Muzzillo, Marina Nitze, Ed Offterdinger, Becky Opp, Jesse Patchett, Jessica Palmer, Carol Pate, Rhodes Perry, Carrie Pierce, Josh & Lauren du Plooy, Andy Polaine, Justin Ponder, Priscilla Price, Melanie Pump, Wesley R.W., Elizabeth Reynolds, Jessica Bott Rosser, Derek Roy, Doug Sandler, Lee Scott, Karla Seidita, Catherine Seow, Austin Smith, Linda Smith, Kim Smith, Ryan Smoot, Sean Soth, Laila Stancioff, Chris Stream, Madalina Tanasescu, James Tesoriero, April Trent, Tom True, Dawn Veselka, Crystal Voight, Shannon Warner, Wendi Washowich, Amy Webber, Marybeth Weiss, Greg Woodard, Laurie Yurchak, Adam Zimmerman

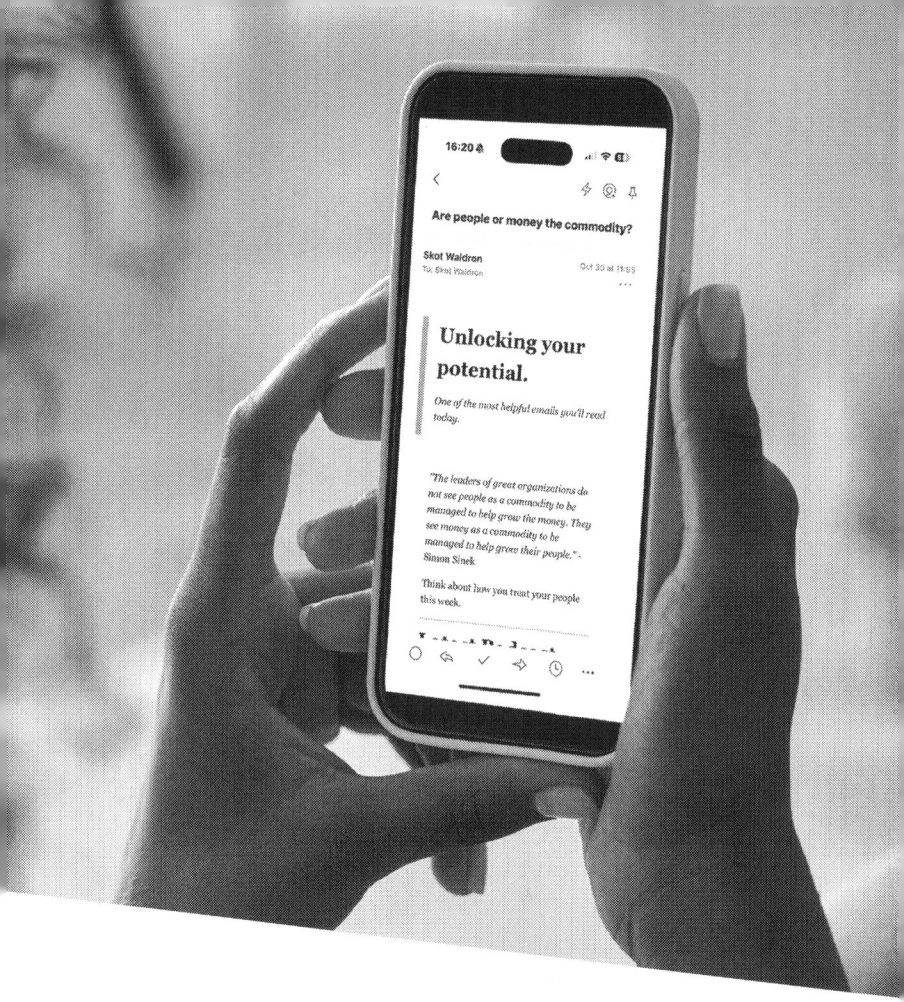

WANT TO FIND WAYS TO CONTINUE UNLOCKING YOUR POTENTIAL EVERY WEEK?

Every Monday, I send a quick thought to set you up for the week. Sometimes, I offer some inspiration, other times it's straight-up application. Regardless, I try to make them the most helpful emails you'll receive that week when it comes to your communication development.

SIGN UP HERE!
Visit skotwaldron.com/email

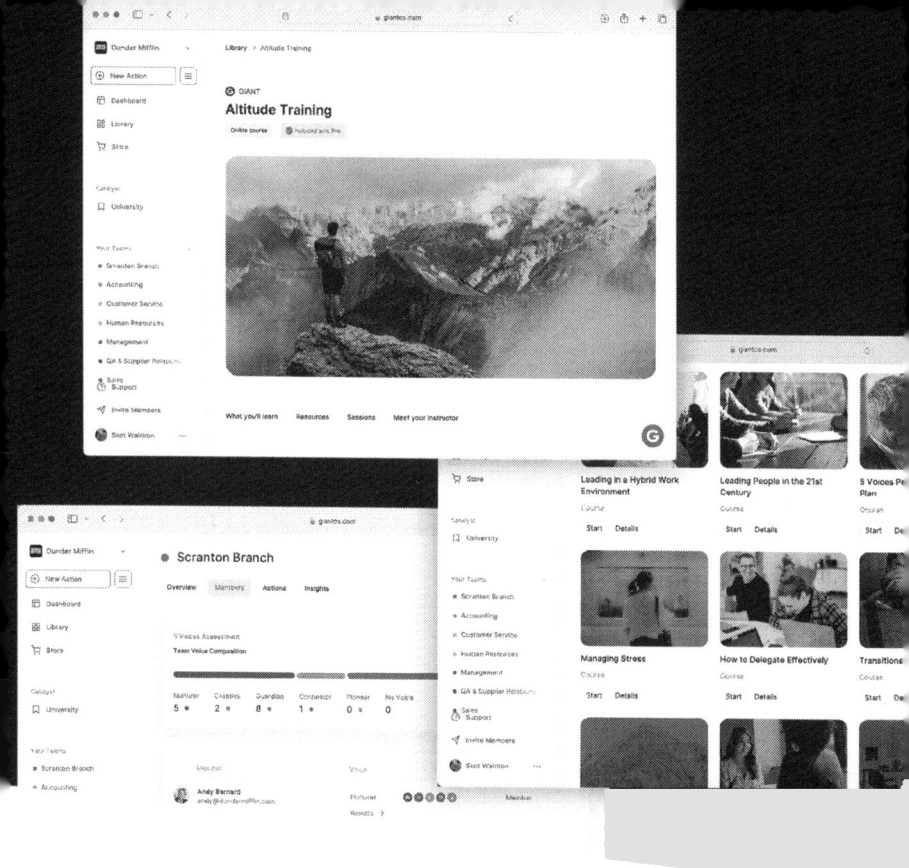

ACCESS TO LEADERSHIP TRAINING, ASSESSMENTS, REPORTS, AND OTHER RESOURCES.

The GiANT Operating System is a simple, on-demand, modern resource for everything you'd need to help you and/or your team communicate better, build more trust, and build more influence.

No contracts. No catch. All of this for $10/mo.

CHECK OUT GIANT!
Visit skotwaldron.com/giant

LOOKING FOR A PODCAST TO HELP UNLOCK YOUR POTENTIAL?

What if there was one place to gain short, powerful insights from influencers worldwide? I interview people like John Lee Dumas of Entrepreneurs on Fire, Ann Hiatt, who worked directly with Jeff Bezos, and Matt Doherty, Michael Jordan's former coach, and I mine the gold inside each of their heads.

LISTEN WHEREVER YOU FIND YOUR PODCASTS!
Visit skotwaldron.com/blog

ATTENDEE STATS:

Found Value: 98%
Reattend Rate: 94%

Main Attributes:
Interactive: 94%
Engaging: 94%
Actionable: 93%
Relevant: 93%
Inspiring: 92%

"Actionable, funny, and easy to listen to."
CONFERENCE ATTENDEE

"People were talking about Skot afterward and wanted him back for the next event which is always great to hear as the planner!"
KOREY ROSALES / SNELL & WILMER

WANT TO SCHEDULE SKOT FOR YOUR NEXT EVENT?

Skot speaks to audiences all over the world. He prides himself on his ability to connect with the planner as well as the attendees. Some of his topics include communication development, managing change, building an intentional leadership brand, and working within a multigenerational workforce.

CONTACT US TO TALK ABOUT YOUR NEXT EVENT!
Visit skotwaldron.com/speaking

Made in the USA
Monee, IL
13 December 2023